LOVE and *POWER:*

The Psychology of Interpersonal Creativity

LOVE and
POWER:

The Psychology of Interpersonal Creativity

Paul Rosenfels, M.D.

LIBRA PUBLISHERS, INC.
NEW YORK, N. Y.

Library of Congress Catalog Card No. 66-25081

© 1966 by Paul Rosenfels, M.D.

LIBRA PUBLISHERS, INC.
1133 Broadway
New York, N. Y. 10010

Manufactured in the United States of America

DEDICATION

In June 1945, standing alone in the Marine cemetery on the island of Tinian in the Marianas, I made a promise to carry throughout life a sense of responsibility for doing my full share to bring a better world into existence. Since then I have turned my back more than once on conventional social responsibility and its rewards to search for the kind of life which might lead to the fulfillment of that pledge. The cemetery in Tinian no longer exists. I offer this book to the memory of the men who once lay buried there.

TABLE OF CONTENTS

PART I. The Mechanisms of Psychological Growth   13

The Psychological Surpluses, 13; Sex and Celebration, 14; Character and Family Life, 16; Character and the External World, 18; The Emergency Reactions, 19; Interpersonal Creativity, 20; Dynamic Imbalance in Character, 21; The Sexual and Celebrative Mechanisms, 23; Truth and Right, 24; Security and Freedom, 25; Faith and Hope, 27; Instincts in the Civilized World, 29; The Sexual and Celebrative Adjustment, 30; The Unstable Equilibrium of the Surpluses, 32; Perversity and Addiction, 33; Withdrawal and Indifference, 35; Idealization and the Exploitation of Reality, 36; The Surpluses and Family Life, 39; The Mated Mechanisms in Family Life, 41; Masculine and Feminine Roles, 42; Masculine and Feminine Tendencies within the Family, 44; The Scope of the Social Roles, 45; Social and Familial Roles, 47; Fantasy and Play-acting, 48; Shame and Guilt, 51; Creativity and the Surpluses, 52; Repression and Renunciation, 54; Psychological Independence and the Surpluses, 57; Creativity and Maturity, 59; The Individual and Social Progress, 61; Aggression and Passivity, 63; The Psychological Content of Interpersonal Creativity, 65; The Mechanisms of Aggression and Passivity, 67; Phobic and Psychopathic Mechanisms, 70; Rebellion and Heresy, 73; Compulsive and Obsessive Mechanisms, 75; Analytic Thinking and Inventive Manipulation, 78; Creative Thinking and Acting, 81

PART II. Creative Maturity   84

Creativity and Social Progress, 84; Maturity and the Surpluses, 86; Adolescence and Maturity, 89; Adolescent Growth and the Mated Mechanisms, 92; Maturity and Depression, 95; Depression and

7

Mental Health, 97; Depression and the Surpluses, 99; The War
Between Men and Women, 102; The War Between Adolescents
and Adults, 106; The Adolescent Community, 107; Adolescence and
Family Life, 111; Adolescence and the Surpluses, 114; The Nature
of the Unattached Surpluses, 117; The Magical and the Miraculous,
120; Adolescent Fantasy and Play-acting, 124; The Search for Nor-
malcy, 127; The Basis of Psychological Independence, 131; Patterns
of Normalcy, 134; Sin and Evil, 137; Idealism and the Sense of
Reality, 141; Autonomy and the Surpluses, 144; Friendship and
Creativity, 147; Homosexuality and Celebrative Partnerships, 150;
The Masculine Community, 154; Inhibition and Perplexity in
Masculine Relationships, 157; Creativity in Masculine Relation-
ships, 161; The Mated Union in Masculine Relationships, 164;
Perversion and Addiction in the Masculine Community, 169

PART III.   Individual Growth and Social Progress   174

Creativity and Social Stability, 174; Contentment and Happiness,
177; The Retreat and the Enlistment, 180; Philosophy and Art, 184;
Human Science and Engineering, 189; Teaching and Leadership
in Education, 191; Psychological Science and Social Control, 196;
Psychotherapy and Social Welfare, 200; Adolescence and Social
Progress, 206; Creativity and Social Instability, 210; Homosexuality
and Social Progress, 215; Prescription for Survival, 221

INDEX   229

LOVE and *POWER:*

The Psychology of Interpersonal Creativity

PART I

THE MECHANISMS OF PSYCHOLOGICAL GROWTH

THE PSYCHOLOGICAL SURPLUSES

A living organism can interact with its environment in one of two ways: by the use of its sensory or responsive capacities or by the exercise of its motor or expressive capacities. The responsive channel of interaction brings data concerning the outside world to the organism. The expressive aspect of interaction confers control over a portion of the external world.

A higher level of interaction with the environment comes into being when a sustained relationship of either the submissive or dominant type is operating. In a submissive relationship, data which has no clear meaning to the organism can alert the entire organism to a higher level of sensibility. It then gathers data selectively as a goal in itself, using mobility where necessary, until the meaning of stimuli becomes clear to the organism. Inner sensations arising from survival needs, such as hunger, alert the whole organism to the gathering of data concerning the sources of food. In a dominant relationship to the environment, energies which have no harmonious pathway for discharge lead the organism to a search for situations which are interesting and productive. The organism commits itself to the finding of opportunity, reaching a higher level of expressiveness. It finds modalities of control by becoming mobile, using selec-

tivity as necessary, until the value of the opportunity becomes apparent. Inner drives arising from survival needs,
such as possession of its food supply, involve the organism
in a permanent commitment to the exercise of skill in manipulative ways.

With the coming of sexuality in the evolutionary development of living organisms, the submissive and dominant
tendencies become specialized in the form of male and
female. In the lower animals such specialization operates
in a significant way only under mated conditions. Before
the courtship and the subsequent union or during non-
mated phases, the submissive or dominant relationships to
the external world are less specialized and are subject to
alteration by external forces and situations. After the reproductive union of male and female, at the evolutionary
level where the young are born immature, the relationship
to the external world shrinks to basic essentials and the
surpluses of tension and energy are expended within the
familial domain, being utilized in the nurture and protection of the young.

SEX AND CELEBRATION

In the mated reproductive relationship in nature, a
domain is formed between male and female in which the
submissive tendency of the female and the dominant tendency of the male have a deepening and invigorating effect
on each other. Depth of feeling for its own sake becomes
sexual, and vigor of attitude for its own sake becomes celebrative. The union of male and female is fulfilled when the
male is drawn into sexuality by means of the sexual intercourse. The male is not feminized by sexual feeling because
his participation has an orgastic goal. As part of the same
mated union, the female participates in the celebrative mood

with the male by means of the mechanism of altruistic surrender. Her surrender to the dominance of the male confines her celebrative mood to the domain which his exercise
of dominance creates, and in this way she is not masculinized
by the experience.

Sexuality is an inborn biological channel of intensification of feeling for its own sake. When this feeling takes
over the whole self, it is no longer directly available for
adaptive interaction with the world, and reaches only toward its own gratification. The celebrative mood, which
is experienced as an untrammeled sense of freedom of the
individual will, is an inborn channel of self-expression, and
when it finds a situation where the individual feels permanently in control without qualification, it reaches only
toward its own further spontaneous expression in a mobile
state colored by pride and exhibitionism. The celebrative
attitude gives an outlet for energy which is not at that
moment available for adaptive use.

In the lower animals the growth process ends with biological maturity. Maturity consists of an endpoint in the
growth process which comes into being when the basis for
interaction with the external world undergoes no further
significant changes. As long as the individual is growing,
the world in which he lives is growing also. The capacity
for further development of the inner life forces does not
end when the world becomes stabilized, however. The capacity for intensification of sensitivity and the expansion
of vigor which are no longer needed to interact with a
growing world becomes channeled into the reproductive
life. Specialization into male and female confers great psychological advantages. A far greater degree of submissiveness is possible where dominance loses access to independent
elaboration, and similarly dominance can reach new heights
of expression where submission is found in dependent chan-

nels only. Each individual pursues his own specialized identity, driven by the biologically established pleasure and enjoyment which these tendencies bring. The courtship is the the time when the differences are manifested and are mutually deepened and invigorated by each other. At the height of these established differences a mating occurs on the basis of a mutual need for each other. They find balance again through each other. The mating relieves each of the tension accumulation and stored energy reserve which court-ship brings. This process repeats itself cyclically until the young arrive at which time female sensitivity is converted into nurture of the young and male vigor is channeled into the establishment of a protective function. The architecture of nature's reproductive mating brings the young into a family domain where the needs of the young can be met at a high level of awareness and involvement.

CHARACTER AND FAMILY LIFE

The specializations which serve to form the structure of the reproductive domain in the lower animals have been used by human beings for a non-reproductive purpose. They form the basis of the creative faculties which civilized man uses to increase his adaptive capacities far above the level which he could otherwise have attained. Civilized man is something new in the evolutionary process. He is more than simply a superior kind of primate. With the emergence of the creative capacities he has become invested with an inner identity which permits lifelong application to conceptual thinking for its own sake and the constructive development of methods and skills as ends in themselves. The character specialization of civilized man makes it possible for him to live in relationship to other human beings in such a way as to increase the adaptive potential of his cerebral cortex many times. Without the high tension levels and large energy reserves which come from specialized human character, there would be no philosophy, science, art, or engineering. It is the capacity for creative productivity which gives man the inner identity which he calls his soul.

Human character becomes specialized for those needs and purposes which have a surplus or creative quality. The creative relationship to the world has as its goal the bringing into existence of new insights and new methods of mastery, which then become the property of all men. There are two fundamental kinds of character, based on the feminine and masculine relationship to life. Since femininity and masculinity of this kind have no direct relationship to the reproductive function, they are not identical with the femininity and masculinity which arise from biological gender. Since men and women must elaborate a social role of masculine or feminine qualities and since this kind of identity is different from the basic character identity, the recognition of the psychological sources of the basic character is often difficult. In this book the basic feminine character, whether in male or female, will be referred to as a yielding character and the corresponding masculine character will be identified as assertive.

In the civilized world the character is formed in either a yielding or assertive pattern by the influence of family life. The family forms and preserves character, operating as a unit in which each member plays an interacting part. The family identity is essential to its permanence and unity. Although the family prepares the growing individual for an ultimate independent relationship with the outer world, it must also serve that side of the individual's needs which has a dependent quality. The dependent needs are different in yielding and assertive families. The yielding family prepares the individual for a life of independent access to understanding while gratifying his dependent needs for access to patterns of action. The assertive family leaves the individual free to explore responsibility on his own while guiding him in a dependent way in the area of beliefs and principles.

CHARACTER AND THE EXTERNAL WORLD

It is man's hunger for knowledge and his sense of self-fulfillment in manipulative skill which have led him to utilize his psychological surpluses in a creative fashion. Through the holding of a reservoir of tension in the form of love for others and the retention of energy potential in the readiness to expend personal power in human affairs, civilized man has made possible a great expansion of human cohesion and cooperation.

The capacity for sustained conceptual thinking takes its psychological origin in the holding of tension in interpersonal relationships, and the development of large scale manipulative procedures begins in the building of energy reserves in human relationships. It is true that the psychological capacities which owe their origin to a love orientation of the self have found their most successful outlet in the non-human subject matters, such as mathematics and physics, but this state of affairs is not due to a lack of psychological investment in the science of human nature, but only to the inherent complexity of the task. Man is a greater builder of skyscrapers and bridges than of effective human institutions, but his striving for constructive social control remains always a primary purpose in life, refractory though the forces of human cooperation may be. In addition to dealing with frustrations in human affairs, civilized man encounters many kinds of inner psychological distortions which arise from the vissicitudes of his creative struggle with the world.

THE EMERGENCY REACTIONS

The specialization of human character into yielding and assertive types arose historically out of a need of the social group for exploration of the unknown and the chaotic in the external world. Before this psychological investment of the self could come into being, men had to deal with the emergency reactions of fear and rage which the unknown and the chaotic arouse. If the unknown is not to arouse fear, the exploration of it must proceed on a basis of inner security in the individual. The only basis for such security lies in the investment of a psychologically feminine surplus for its own sake. If the chaotic is not to invoke rage, the effort to deal with it must be characterized by a sense of freedom in the individual. The only source of this kind of personal freedom lies in the utilization of a psychologically masculine surplus as an end in itself. Inner security of a surplus kind becomes the basis of truth seeking, and surplus psychological freedom leads to the elaboration and extension of the right. In the context of this book, the right refers to that state of possession of the modalities of control which is characterized by inner pride and a sense of integrity, and uses resources in such a way as to bring out their inherent and ultimate qualities. The right has no goals but its own effectiveness, and it is unalloyed with destructiveness.

The emergency reactions utilize surplus mechanisms for survival purposes. The same unlimited capacity for feeling and self-awareness which enters the sexual channel in reproduction can be converted by circumstances into fear. The individual is receptive to sexuality when his expanding self-awareness is harmonious and pleasurable, but the expanding self-awareness of fear is discordant and painful, leading him to take flight from danger. The unlimited readiness for mobility and self-confidence which leads to the celebrative mood can be converted by circumstances into

rage. The individual welcomes the celebrative state because
the expanding self-confidence is characterized by spontaneous
enjoyment, but he enters into conflict with his environment
in the presence of rage because the stresses produce intoler-
able suffering.

INTERPERSONAL CREATIVITY

In the social interaction of civilized human beings a
maximum of depth and scope is sought for its own sake.
When men interact on such a basis, they are in a position
to deal with human problems and obstacles, and social life
becomes an expanding entity which makes room for personal growth. The development of social cohesion and
cooperation ultimately alters established social ideas and
institutions, resulting in social progress. The individual
finds a place for psychological growth because the world
around him is well supplied with the stimulating challenges
which his idealizing nature and possessive tendencies require.

When the personality is balanced, reacting with submissive or dominant tendencies which are the opposite of the
basic character, the individual finds himself completely taken
up by his adaptive involvement with the world. When the
individual meets the world with a surplus within himself,
choosing those relationships which reinforce and express
his specialized character, he has greater access to contentment
and happiness. The surplus interface between the individual
and society is enlarged by selectivity and mobility in interpersonal relationships. The yielding surplus is recognized
as love; the assertive surplus takes the form of personal
power.

When the growing individual has reached his biological
maturity, the surpluses emerge in their sexual and celebrative form and are utilized among the lower animals for
the formation of the domain. The domain has as its func-

tion the rearing of the young. Civilized human beings use
love and power to maintain a state of psychological growth
throughout life. It is the capacity for growth in interpersonal
relationships which elevates the civilized individual above
the level of both the lower animals and the primitive in
his own nature. Growth not only implies an expansion of
self-awareness and self-confidence within the self, but also
a deeping understanding and an increasing capacity for
responsibility in interpersonal relationships. The individual
and his world grow together, and this process leaves a resi-
due of knowledge and ability behind which outlives the
life span of the individual. Love is meaningless unless it
does work in the world; power is without enduring value
unless it finds constructive opportunity. As love does its
work in human relationships, it produces insights which
are readily communicable and become the property of all.
As power finds its proper outlets, it becomes capable of
exercising leadership, and its techniques are passed from
one generation to another through identification with the
modalities of mastery. Insights which come from the hands
of love and mastery which evolves from the devoted commitments of personal power become the tools of social
progress.

DYNAMIC IMBALANCE IN CHARACTER

Love which governs the surplus relationship of the individual to his world alters the character in a feminine
direction and leaves the self in a state of dynamic imbalance.
The individual bears a harmonious tension in his relationships with others, seeking always to expand the depth of
this interaction, because such feelings give him a sense of
increased self identity. If he is to remain healthy, he must
bear tension in such a way that it can ultimately be discharged. With each successful discharge, he is more able

to renew the tension accumulation without fear of being overwhelmed by it. The individual sacrifices independent access to freedom of action in order to find the kind of inner security which opens his personality to depth of feeling without arbitrary limit.

Personal power which governs the surplus relationship of the individual to his world alters the character in a masculine direction, resulting in a dynamically unbalanced personality. The individual carries a surplus of energy in the form of a potential for action, seeking always to expand the scope of the vigor he invests in his personal interactions. This kind of self-expression heightens his mood in a self-fulfilling way. If he is to retain his capacity for social conformity, he must use his energies in such a way that they find socially constructive channels of expression. With each success in establishing an outlet, he is more able to renew the energy accumulation without danger of encountering social conflict in the process. In the surplus area where personal power operates, the individual sacrifices independent access to secure self-awareness in favor of unlimited freedom of action.

Wherever the surplus tendencies are found, whether it is in the reproductive life of the mated union in nature or in the creative interpersonal life of civilized man, they bring a dependent need for the finding of balance. The domain draws a circle around two interacting individuals who find permanence and completeness together; they have no further relationship with the world except to satisfy basic needs or to deal with emergencies. In creative relationships the surplus tendencies lead out into the world. Love holds its tensions until it finds work to do in the service of others, and such activity brings balance and relief from mounting tension. Power maintains its potential for action until it finds constructive opportunity which has social meaning, and when it finds such a commitment the feeling of involvement brings balance, creating avenues of discharge for the mounting energy accumulations. The mastery patterns of love are never ends in themselves. They accomplish their tasks, and are then laid aside while love prepares itself for further work. The attachments of power depend on the insights contained in the individual's view of his world, but this sense of meaning is never sought as an end in itself. The insights accumulated by power provide outlets for action, and when these needs have been gratified by the full exploitation of opportunity, the individual turns toward the exploration of new interests and loyalties.

THE SEXUAL AND CELEBRATIVE MECHANISMS

The reproductive surplus which forms the domain in the lower animals first manifests itself in the courtship period. The submissiveness of the female is stirred by the dominance of the male, and male dominance is aroused in the process. As feminine depth of feeling increases without limit, it becomes channeled biologically into sexual feeling, and masculine vigor overflows into the celebrative mood. Each partner then finds balance through the sharing of the other's state of being, utilizing empathy and identification. Balance is reached through a dependent relationship with the partner. When male sexuality is aroused by the female it has an orgastic goal. The tension accumulation is guaranteed a biological outlet in the act of copulation and therefore does not feminize the male. When the female celebrative state is brought into being by the behavior of the male it takes its origin in the surrender to masculine control, and feminine mobility is confined to the area where the male is in command. Within this domain, and in the company of the male, the female is free to discharge energy for its own sake. This pattern of utilization of the biological channels of celebrative energy discharge does not masculinize the female.

In the mated union, masculine warmth must be sexualized if the masculine identity is to be preserved, and feminine pride must enter celebrative channels if the feminine identity is to remain intact. With the arrival of the young, sex and celebration depart in favor of the nurturing and protecting functions. The mechanisms of this stage of the reproductive life have been used by civilized mankind in building love and power in interpersonal relationships. In this final stage of the reproductive union, male warmth flows toward the female and the young, but not in surplus; it is not a limitless feelingfulness. Female pride is aroused by the inclusion of the male and the young in her world, but it is not an attitude based on unlimited access to action. Female warmth, however, is in surplus, and is available to the young in the ministration to their needs. Male pride is also in surplus, guaranteeing a maximum readiness to protect the safety of the young from all outside threats to their security. By this method, nature has given the offspring an environment of the greatest possible survival value.

TRUTH AND RIGHT

The desexualized and non-celebrative surpluses which are expended in the domain of the mated union are available to creative interpersonal relationships in the civilized world. This shift of direction eliminates the domain with its separation from the world outside, and brings man close to a sense of the magical and miraculous in his dealings with other people. Behind this utilization of the surpluses in human relationships lies man's religious spirit and his sense of fervor in group undertakings. Without a social investment of the surpluses the meaning and value of life diminishes, losing enthusiasm and inspiration, and men become subject to the invasive depredations of flattened affect and depression of mood.

The surplus embodied in creative love needs work to do but it cannot expend itself in willful power without destroying the substance and depth of love. The willfulness which channels the work of love lies outside the individual and resides in the thing loved. The person who loves must find his avenues of action through a dependent relationship with the forces in society which embody the kind of power he can believe in. If he attempts to find what is right purely out of his own inner resources, his access to truth is compromised. The tension accumulating life of creative love does not take a sexual channel, but accumulates insight and truth as its natural destiny.

The surplus invested in creative power needs attachments and loyalties, but it cannot be captured by a self-conscious awareness without undermining the scope and spontaneity of power. The image of the self which comes to the individual out of his awareness of his possessions must take its origins outside the self, originating in the responsiveness of the environment. The individual who is the vehicle of personal power must find feelingfulness through a dependent relationship with the sources of love in society which are worthy of his loyalty. If he attempts to find the truth exclusively out of his own inner resources, his access to the right is compromised. The energy accumulating life of creative power does not find discharge through celebrative experience, but accumulates mastery and right as its inevitable goal.

SECURITY AND FREEDOM

If love is to be creative in nature, it must attach itself in a selective manner. When love commits itself where there is no need of its unlimited depth, it is divested of its surplus quality. The truth seeking function of love seeks to reduce the unknown in human affairs, and for this the individual must be able to believe in the ultimate emergence of the insights which can win territory from the unknown. The only way he can know that this state of affairs exists is through his idealizing capacities. The individual cannot solve problems in human relationships without the kind of involvements with other people which lead to exposure to new experiences. Although he is guided on this path by the spirit of love itself, seeking to deepen understanding for its own sake, he must find a submissive participation in what he believes to be right. The activities of those who embody the right are idealized by him. As he works within the area established by the right, he finds inner security and peace of mind, whether understanding has yet emerged or not. Unless the understanding he seeks takes its origin within the domain of the right, it loses access to social meaning and becomes a mere exercise in self-serving intellectuality. Human insights come to the thinker when the creative interaction with others has done its work. They do not emerge because he has a need for the release of inner tension or because of their potential adaptive usefulness.

Personal power operates in a mobile fashion in its creative phases. If power accepts involvement where there is no opportunity for the investment of its expansive nature, the surplus in it will be undermined. The reaching for the right is a function of power, and it involves itself with the chaotic in human affairs under circumstances where control is within the scope of ultimate attainment. This state of affairs can only exist where the individual is able to feel an unassailable confidence in the ultimate emergence of those modalities of mastery which can win territory from the chaotic. He will only find himself in this psychological state when the human environment becomes his reality, that is, when his explorations of mastery techniques are guided by actual human responses. In this process he is accessible to a deepening awareness of the human resources at hand. He is motivated in this undertaking by the spirit of power, reaching for an expansion of responsibility for its own sake. The new awareness and feelingfulness that come to him do not arise from an inner self-awareness, but from a sense of the possession of the truth. The ideas of those who are the carriers of truth become his assets. As he reaches toward self-expression within the area defined by truth, he finds inner freedom and spontaneity of action whether the capacity to take responsibility has yet emerged or not. Unless the capacity for responsibility that he attempts to develop has taken root in the domain of truth, it loses social value and becomes a mere embellishment and display of vanity. Human mastery can emerge only when the efforts of the individual have been tempered in the forge of uncompromising human involvement. It does not come because the energy accumulation of the individual calls for discharge, or because of the adaptive advantages which might ensue.

FAITH AND HOPE

The capacity of love to hold tension is essential to its existence. When love is desexualized it no longer has a biological channel of discharge. If tension mounts in a meaningless fashion, the individual cannot maintain his mental health. The resolution of the tensions of love comes out of its accomplishments in human affairs, and especially out of the insights which result from the search for understanding. The release from problem solving effort brings a harmonious and pleasurable psychological state of self-awareness which is characterized by contentment. Love must be prepared for any task which its own sensitivity and perceptiveness establishes, and once started on a course of action, its labors may

be Herculean in scope and without guarantee of success in
any given time and place. Love is willing to pay the price
of such devoted effort. The work of love brings a diminution
in self-awareness, and in this phase the tension level of love
is maintained by faith. Faith is essential if love is to leave
behind the secure orientation of established insights to go
forth into an unprotected world of experience. Faith permits
security to enter the self, becoming a permanent asset of
the personality, above and beyond the vissicitudes of the life
of experience.

The capacity of power to accumulate energy is essential
to its existence. When power gives up its celebrative investment, it no longer finds an automatic biological channel
for energy utilization. If accumulated energy finds no outlets of value, the individual cannot maintain his social conformity. The finding of outlets comes through the making
of meaningful human attachments, and especially out of the
mastery which evolves from the reaching for responsibility.
The release from the search for meaning brings a harmonious and enjoyable psychological state of self-confidence
which is characterized by a sense of happiness. Personal
power must be ready to expose itself to any kind of tension
bearing which its own vigor and resourcefulness requires,
and once committed to extremes of discipline, its selflessness
may be Promethean in scope without guarantee of effectiveness in any particular time and place. Power accepts the
cost of such self-developing involvements, not resisting the
constriction of self-confidence which such submission brings.
In this phase of its operation the energy level of power is
maintained by hope. When hope shapes the goals of human
undertakings, power can put aside the immediate rewards
of freedom without losing its inner identity. Hope establishes freedom as the organizing principle of the personality,
insuring the integrity of power regardless of the circumstances of day to day commitments.

INSTINCTS IN THE CIVILIZED WORLD

Character specialization of the yielding or assertive type takes priority over the biological specialization into male or female. Nature has organized the instinctual tendencies in such a way that their form can be molded by the context in which they come into being. If instinctual patterns are not reinforced, the drive behind them tends to become generalized, and alterations develop in the pathways of expression. The sexual and celebrative instincts of male and female in nature come to fruit in an environment which facilitates the submissive role of the female and the dominant role of the male. The sexual and celebrative instincts of civilized man come to their mature expression in a world in which some persons are already committed to a yielding role in life, and others to an assertive role. These commitments are strongly reinforced by social contexts and have an impelling importance in the maintenance of the inner identity. If the individual attempts to give up his character identity in favor of his biological identity, the whole basis of his mental health and social conformity is compromised. Men care more for their sense of individuality and the rewarding depth and vigor which it brings than they do for uncomplicated conformity to their biological role. If they turn away from the complexities of character differentiation, they cheat themselves of the psychological heritage which is the basis of civilization itself. They become the victims of a glorification of biological identity which leads them on into a wasteland of ignorance and pretense. Without character specialization their interpersonal relationships can never develop the richness and scope which the apparent vividness of their biological identity has led them to expect.

Men learn to adhere to their inner identity out of the search for contentment and happiness. Adolescence in the

civilized world is more than a time of adjustment to emerging biological maturity. It is a time of affirmation and re-
affirmation of the inner identity in relationship to the
world, and it constitutes a search for the self which requires
both time and space for the reaching of its fulfillment. The
search is not terminated with absolute finality even when a
stable pattern of mature social adjustment is attained.
Adolescent mechanisms are subject to reemergence whenever the impact of major human problems and obstacles
exposes the individual to an inescapable need for inner
growth.

THE SEXUAL AND CELEBRATIVE ADJUSTMENT

Sex and celebration have a place in the psychological life
of civilized man which is unique in the evolutionary scale.
The mated mechanisms which bring the psychological surpluses into being are no longer contained within the reproductive domain. Desexualized love and non-celebrative
power constitute the major psychological content of man's
civilized existence. If the surpluses enter where they do
not belong, man's most cherished human goals become impossible of attainment. The task of the developing personality is the establishment of a place for sex and celebration which is walled off from areas where it does not belong,
while maintaining a full access to intensity and spontaneity.
Man is the only animal who is called upon to make an
adjustment to his own surplus tendencies. He deals with
sex and celebration as things in themselves which appear
and disappear without apparent design or means of control,
becoming threats to his equilibrium or gifts from the hands
of life, depending on the context in which they are experienced. The adolescent search for an inner identity must
include the finding of a place within the personality for the
sexual and celebrative life.

The sexual adjustment reaches toward stability and does not welcome the problems inherent in the unknown. It rejects tasks of any sort, save the biologically channeled activity which serves its own physical gratification. In order to find the simple organic patterns of sexual arousal which physical love needs, the individual has to be able to set up contexts in his personal life where such phenomena can readily occur. The finding of these contexts is the key to the sexual adjustment. They are subject to great variation in the life of different individuals, as well as variation in different phases of the mature life of the same individual, depending on the pressures of his own psychological growth. No individual can accept psychological growth without risking a shift in his sexual adjustment. Each individual wants to take a good sexual adjustment for granted, and the bringing of sexuality into focus as a problem in itself comes only as a psychological necessity. Sexual adjustment has become one of the elements in man's adaptive world, being inextricably involved with his mental health. It is only important as a thing in itself when the contexts it needs cannot readily be found.

Celebrative personal power, in contrast to the creative outlets of power, does not attempt to find its fulfillment in chaotic situations. It rejects any commitments which would lower its elevated mood. Feelings flow only into those situations which give automatic outlet to its high spirits. In order to find the necessary simple spontaneity on which celebration rests, the individual has to establish contexts in his personal life which guarantee such outlets. The finding of these contexts is the key to the celebrative adjustment, and they must be found by each individual in accordance with his personal needs. Such contexts are subject to change in the presence of psychological growth. The attainment of established patterns of mood elevation is something that each individual would like to take for granted. The estab-

lishing of socially harmonious celebrative outlets has become
one of man's adaptive necessities without which his social
conformity is undermined. Celebration only becomes important as a thing in itself when the contexts which it
needs cannot readily be found.

THE UNSTABLE EQUILIBRIUM OF THE SURPLUSES

Man must make a sexual and celebrative adjustment
through the finding of contexts which preserve sexual
potency and celebrative self-abandonment without the
undermining of creative interpersonal relationships. For
this purpose society brings into being general patterns of
permissiveness and prohibitions which are supported by
social ideas and institutions. Although society establishes
certain limits, the development of an adequate sexual and
celebrative life remains the ultimate psychological task of
the individual. Since adequate sexuality takes its being in
privacy and is characterized by an unlimited feelingfulness,
it is not directly under social influence. Its boundaries are
established through the regulation of the contexts which
arouse it. Celebration takes place in the social world, but it
is detached and separate from adaptive commitments, and
since its mood must be unlimited in quality it is intolerant
of direct social control. There are no fixed patterns for
the development of an adequate and socially acceptable
sexual and celebrative adjustment. In a healthy personality
there is always room for further exploration of sexual pleasure, provided that it proves acceptable to the self, just as
there are no necessary commitments to sexuality where its
disappearance does no harm to the self. In a socially harmonious personality there is always readiness for an expansion of
celebrative enjoyment which proves acceptable to the self,
just as there can be no fixed need of celebrative expression
in any given aspect of living. The psychological surpluses

are therefore in an unstable equilibrium and are phasic in the life of the individual, expanding and contracting according to his efforts to come to terms with this side of his nature. Literally, the work of adapting to sex and celebration is never finished. Sexual love tends to be blind, and celebrative power tends to exhibitionistic excesses. The mature personality tolerates his irrationalities and impulsiveness in this area as part of the acceptance of his human qualities.

PERVERSITY AND ADDICTION

Sexuality may be healthy or unhealthy, and the ultimate test of the contexts in which sexuality is aroused is not a matter of social standards but of the inner equilibrium of the personality. Perversity is sexuality that feeds on itself. It has an autistic quality, erecting a barrier within the self which makes celebrative experience difficult to find.

Celebration may be socially harmonious or antisocial. The contexts which bring it into being are selected by the individual out of his need to fulfill himself and not through any automatic acceptance of social beliefs. Addiction to power moods is celebration which rejects social interests and surrenders to its own euphoric world. Its presence makes sexuality difficult to find.

Sexuality cannot form a healthy bond between two human beings in and of itself. It must depend on the context in which it emerges for its meaningful status. In the mated state in nature the context is created by the domain. Feminine depth of feeling is aroused by male vigor, and when deepening feeling spills over into the sexual channel, the female carries the male with her into the act of copulation.

The celebrative state cannot be the exclusive basis of an interpersonal relationship without becoming antisocial. It is dependent on context for its attainment of social value. In the domain the mated relationship enlivens male vigor in the presence of feminine sensitivity. When masculine energy breaks free into the celebrative sphere, it includes the female through the mechanism of her altruistic surrender.

Family life in the civilized world is built out of relationships which are not mated in the biological sense and which do not form a domain. The partners bring an existent sexual and celebrative capacity to each other and share together on an equal basis the pleasure and enjoyment of their surplus psychological life. The establishment of contexts in which sex and celebration are neither over-controlled or over-expressed in the lives of the partners is crucial to the success of the relationship.

Sexual feeling which responds only to the sexual nature of another person is perverse, and unmated sexuality is vulnerable to perverse manifestations. When love governs the feelings of the individual, becoming permissive of sexuality in certain contexts, perversity can be overcome because love is capable of making a place for the power needs of the partners. This opens the door to celebrative experience and guarantees the balance of the psychological surpluses. A celebrative attitude which involves itself only with a similar attitude in another is addicted in nature, and unmated celebration is vulnerable to addictive phenomena. When power establishes the mood of the individual, making a place for celebrative experience in certain contexts, the addiction pattern can be overcome because power can take responsibility for the love needs of the partners. This gives access to sexuality and guarantees psychological balance.

Whenever sex and celebration exist in a non-mated state, only love and power are big enough to contain them and establish circumstances in which they can reach fulfillment. This kind of love and power is actually desexualized and non-celebrative. It is permissive of sex and celebration, but it does not owe its existence to them. Any time love comes into being through sexuality instead of love granting a place to sexuality, invasion of the personality by perverse phenomena becomes inevitable. If power owes its existence to the celebrative state instead of celebration being released by power, addiction tendencies will become established within the personality. The ultimate cause of perversity is the inability to become fully involved by desexualized love, and addiction is rooted in the inability to commit the self to a non-celebrative power world. In the barren land where love and power cannot grow, depression is kept at bay by the overgrowth of perversity and addiction, and men convince themselves that this garden of weeds is their natural heritage.

WITHDRAWAL AND INDIFFERENCE

The establishment of a specialized character creates an imbalance within the self. One of the functions of family life is to satisfy the dependent needs of the individual for balance. The access to equilibrium is essential to mental health and social harmony. As the individual turns from the family to the outer world, the mated mechanisms tend to come into play. Depth in the yielding character is enriched in the presence of an assertive ideal, and vigor in the assertive character is enlivened by the responsiveness of the yielding elements in his social environment.

Individuals who develop a deeper and broader character identity than their familial environment can accept and support are driven to an autonomous search for self-realization in interaction with the outer world. The first step in breaking away from family influence in a yielding environment is withdrawal. The individual cuts himself off from the dependent support which the family offers for his assistance in reaching experience. If he is not to fall victim to neurotic inhibition he must find sufficient mobility to

enter a new psychological environment on his own. Once
he has established an inner identity consistent with his
needs, he can begin again to make familial-type attachments. The transitional period is one of inner growth and
it is adolescent in nature. His mobility is in the service
of his search for an ideal. In some individuals this search
never ends and they live permanently in a pattern of rebellion and cynicism.

The first step in the breaking away from family influence
in an assertive environment is the refusal to feel em-
pathetically with others. This state of indifference cuts off the
individual from dependency on familial ideas and beliefs.
If he is not to fall victim to delinquent perplexity, he must
find sufficient discrimination and selectivity to develop his
own loyalties in a new psychological environment. Once he
has found an inner identity worthy of his strivings, he
can afford to make familial-type attachments again. His
selectivity has as its goal the discovery of a responsive human
environment which can embody reality for him. Some
individuals never discover such a world and they retain
their individuality only through heretical disbelief and
opportunism.

IDEALIZATION AND THE EXPLOITATION
OF REALITY

If love is to do creative work in the world, it must have
the capacity for idealization. The establishment of an ideal
is a conceptual process. The ideal is an entity which maintains an unassailable unity no matter what problems
emerge in the course of an interaction with it. The individual remains aware of his own permanent submissive relationship to it. Idealization is a feeling state of esthetic
quality, and the ideal embodies beauty.

If power is to find a constructive outlet for its manipulative capacities, it must be able to exploit the inherent malleability of resources. Such resources are not discovered conceptually; they become real to the individual out of experience. The interaction with reality is a matter of dealing with the concrete. Reality has a permanent identity, and no matter what obstacles emerge in the course of a manipulative relationship with it, the sense of possession which permanence brings is never broken. A sense of reality comes to the individual as an aspect of experiencing what is right and is ethical in nature. Reality embodies goodness, creating an environment worth possessing.

The adolescent struggle to establish an inner identity requires that the individual find his ideal or his sense of reality outside the family circle. The family has given him his specialized character and the dependent support he needs to find balance, but he has not yet used his inner identity in an autonomous relationship with the world. He cannot fulfill his need to contribute to the reservoir of truth and right on which social progress rests unless he is able to go beyond the concepts and methods of the previous generation. To do this, he must find his own inter-action with the ideal and his own sense of reality. If the family rejects his efforts to establish a creative relationship with the outside world, he will need rebellion and heresy to reach this autonomy.

Whether idealization is directed toward human beings or toward impersonal entities, it utilizes love as its vehicle. Without love idealization cannot reach the kind of inter-action which permits growth and the winning of territory from the unknown. Whether the reaching for a wider reality takes place in a human or impersonal environment, it utilizes personal power as its instrument. Without power the sense of reality cannot explore life in a way that pre-serves its capacity for growth and permits the individual to deal with the chaotic.

Man has made his greatest creative contributions in impersonal areas. His love of the world has brought enriching insights in the area of science, and his power relationships have bestowed rewarding mastery in the area of engineering techniques. Desexualized love and non-celebrative power have found their first and easiest application in the non-human fields of endeavor. These accomplishments have come at some psychological cost to the human being, because they often exact the price of a constriction in the depth and scope of human interpersonal reactions. The ivory tower of the intellectual is no accident. Without it, he would have to risk his wisdom in the market place of daily living, dealing with problems which involve him personally and exposing the unknown in himself. The commitment of the man of action to the harnessing of the forces of nature has spared him a full scale exposure to inner moral conflict. Without the outlet which the undertaking of impressive works and hazardous tasks affords, his strength would have to be tested in the arena of the commonplace in human affairs, dealing with obstacles that involve his personal life and engaging the chaotic within himself.

When love is directed toward an idealized human being, the sexuality in that individual becomes part of what is known. If the relationship is not to be sexualized, it is necessary that it fully express that kind of human interaction which mutually serves the inner identity, and there is no limit on the amount of understanding and responsibility which can be invested. It must be guided only by the need of each to deepen and expand his interaction with society.

When personal power finds outlet in an attachment to a responsive human being, the submissive celebrative tendencies become part of the human reality. If the relationship is not to be taken over by the celebrative spirit, it is necessary for it to be guided into channels which serve the psychological growth of both individuals, and there is no fixed limit on the amount of understanding and responsibility which may be invested.

Love and power are in great need of each other if they are not to be cut off from the roots which feed their depth and vigor. In their development they must pass through an area fraught with sexual and celebrative dangers. Adolescence is the time when the personality first comes to grip with these great psychological issues. If sexuality and celebration are too easily conquered in human growth relationships, love may lose its capacity to find a living human ideal, and power may be cut off from the sources of genuine human opportunity. If the surpluses usurp the place of goodness and beauty in a permanent way, men find themselves unable to reach a creative relationship with society, and must accept withdrawal and indifference as an inevitable part of their psychic life.

THE SURPLUSES AND FAMILY LIFE

The warmth and cooperation of family life utilize love and power in a stable fashion. Although the family must establish a specialized yielding or assertive atmosphere if the individual is to have an inner identity, the family as such does not seek to grow psychologically. Its purposes are served by reinforcement of the familiar and adherence to the reliable. It prepares its growing members for a life of independent adult psychological growth, and makes a place for the adult members to interact with the outside world on a creative level. It provides for balance within the personality of its members so that tension and energy do not accumulate in an environment which cannot utilize an excess of these psychological states. The family wants love, but not more than serves its interests. It makes a place for power, but only as much as the existent family loyalties can fulfill. It is very important that family attachments have a desexualized and non-celebrative basis. Since the family is the giver of mental health and the arbiter of social harmony, it must ultimately concern itself with the sexual and celebrative components of the personality. It accomplishes this end by taking cognizance of sexuality which already exists, and dealing with celebrative tendencies which are ready to express themselves. The family establishes contexts of a private and separate nature in which sex and celebration run their course, and these contexts remain isolated from the main stream of familial interaction. This kind of sex and celebration has an adaptive basis. The contexts are established by mutual exploration, consent, and arrangement. Sex, which is not inherently rational, is given a rational home. Celebration, which is not inherently subject to organization, is released in a disciplined way.

Too much order and organization can destroy sex and celebration. Sexual potency and celebrative self-abandonment cannot be sacrificed without damage to mental health and social harmony. Civilized familial sexuality is no longer feminine and masculine in the primitive biological sense, but rather has as its goal a balanced sexuality between two partners, each with a capacity to store sexual tension, and each with orgastic capacity. The civilized celebrative strivings no longer follow the mated patterns of nature, but rather utilize the capacity of each partner to store celebrative energy and release it by a mutual and cooperating surrender.

The mated mechanisms are never far from the surface in the search for sexual potency and celebrative self-abandonment, and this fact has no necessary connection with the biological gender of the partners. In either heterosexual or homosexual relationships, the psychological femininity of men and the psychological masculinity of women can readily be used in the pursuit of sexual and celebrative adequacy. The inner character, when well defined, is always dominant over biological identity under civilized conditions. If the character fails to attain clear definition, and men turn toward their biological identity in an attempt to establish a valid inner nature, they attain only a caricature of primitive potency and self-abandonment which becomes self-defeating in human relationships.

THE MATED MECHANISMS IN FAMILY LIFE

The familial surpluses express themselves in a time and place chosen for them by rational and disciplined human beings. The yielding personality is dependent in the expression of the masculine side of the surplus tendencies. The partners help each other to find the masculine components together. What each needs is another individual who supplies the masculine component as it is used in the reaching of balance, and this does not imply a masculine personality. Men who elaborate a deep capacity for tension bearing in a creative pattern often choose wives who are actionists in domestic life and casual social activities, but who are in no sense masculine in their inner identity.

The assertive personality is dependent in the expression of the feminine side of his surplus tendencies. He must find empathetic communication with a partner who embodies the feminine patterns he needs. This feminine component is a contribution to the relationship and does not imply a feminine personality. He finds another assertive personality who is oriented toward loyalty and attachment in such a way as to enlarge the interpersonal cohesion of both. Men who are creative at the action level often find wives who embody feminine virtues in domestic life and casual social activities, but who retain a clear masculine identity in the inner self.

The psychological welfare of the family requires that the dependent needs of its adult members be met with a maximum of effectiveness. Courtship provides a testing

ground for the establishment of mutually beneficial dependent relationships. Although men must elaborate a
masculine social role, and women a feminine one, the way
in which they accept masculine and feminine tendencies
toward each other is governed by their need to reach a stable
equilibrium together. Whichever partner is best suited to
maintain heightened tension or energy levels for both
performs this function, and the other maintains their mutual
access to discharge of these surpluses. In a good marital
relationship, one partner is more autonomous in his character development, and the other is more dependent in type.

MASCULINE AND FEMININE ROLES

The domestic household established by family life needs
stability and reliability. It is a social institution which
society protects because its child-rearing function serves the
interests of society. Only certain general characteristics are
established by social influences. Within this broad social
identity there is room for the marital partners to create the
kind of interaction which best serves their personal needs.
The actual nature of the masculine and feminine role within
the family is subject to wide variance in the private and
separate psychological life. These roles are important to the
individual in a dual way. In relationship to society in
general the masculine and feminine roles must be well-
defined according to gender in conventional terms, sufficient
to establish the image of a stable marriage which bears
significant similarities to other marriages. It is a way of
universalizing marriage and giving it a social identity which
can exist without regard for individual differences. The
second way in which the masculine and feminine roles
are important is in the personal surplus interaction between
the marital partners. Here the identity of each must be
found out of their shared personal needs, and the role they

play has no necessary relationship to the social one. Courtship before marriage is often prolonged and experimental
in nature. This courtship is different from the mated courtship of animals. Its purpose is not to release the inborn
masculine and feminine tendencies, but rather to discover
the interpersonal contexts in which the partners feel com-
fortable and interested in a shared life which includes the
surplus tendencies. They explore the question of their
capacity for warmth and cooperation together, without
the inevitable intrusion of sex and celebration, while making
provision for a time and place in which the surplus pleasures and enjoyments can be accepted and reach their fulfillment.

The complexities of civilized courtship are far greater
than in the case of mated courtship. The spirit of romance
and adventure infuses longing and eagerness into the surplus
life. Romance must be cultivated by the partners. If the
enthusiasm is not there, it cannot be forced on the relationship. The sense of adventuresome inspiration which they
share must flow readily from their natural interests, and
cannot be artificially constructed. Although they choose the
contexts in which the surpluses are expressed, they are not
privileged to alter each other in order to attain these outlets. A marriage which is based primarily on social advantages, in which each partner embodies a high level of
excellence in the social image of what a wife or husband
is supposed to be, but where the marriage has failed from
the beginning to take interaction at the surplus level into
account, can never tolerate privacy and separateness. It is
also true that a marriage which was formed exclusively
out of the romantic and adventuresome spirit, without due
regard for the adaptive relationship of the family to the
rest of society, must always gravitate toward privacy and
separateness and thus fail to sustain the necessary social
identity.

The masculine and feminine roles in relationship to
society are established by the acceptance of conventional
gender traits, which are based partly on biological tendencies of a general nature but take their essential form through
the influence of social ideas and institutions. The conformity to community standards of masculinity and femininity at a minimal level is essential to social empathy and
acceptance. When the creative feminine tendencies of men
gain expression in the adaptive area where they do not
belong, they interfere with the elaboration of the masculine
social role and the personality becomes effete. Where the
creative masculine tendencies are overinvested in the masculine social role, the personality becomes brutalized.

MASCULINE AND FEMININE TENDENCIES
WITHIN THE FAMILY

In a familial partnership between individuals of like
character, the absence of primitive mated mechanisms creates difficulties in the establishment of sexual and celebrative
outlets. As the partners seek to make a place for their surplus tendencies, they use their masculine and feminine
traits in any way that contributes to sexual and celebrative
gratification. For this purpose one partner tends to take
either a tension or energy holding role, and the other provides the opposite to the degree that is required to achieve
balance. This division into feminine and masculine is for
the limited purpose of finding surplus pleasure and enjoyment. It is a psychological arrangement which takes its
being in the personal relationship between the partners and
can only fulfill itself in the context of that relationship.
It is not bound to gender, as is the masculine and feminine
identity of the social roles. It comes from those pairings
established by courtship in which psychological functions
are accepted without regard to which one is male or female.

This is not a mated relationship because both partners face the outside world with the same type of inner character and in their adaptive life they share a common view of life and way of life. It is a means of enriching and invigorating the surplus life and belongs in this private and separate world. It must not alter the masculine or feminine social role or distort the basic inner character.

In those cases where the social role is so rigid as to completely dominate familial psychological functions, there is no need for courtship and no guarantee that the partners will find a spirit of romance and adventure together. Such a dominating social role tends to invade the inner character and is destructive of creative relationships between the individual and the outer world.

THE SCOPE OF THE SOCIAL ROLES

Unless love does work in the world it cannot fulfill itself. The feminine social role as it is utilized in the adaptive functions of family life cannot lead to a growing productive interaction with society. It must be stable and reliable and it rejects growth as a potential threat to its continuity. The tasks that come out of its functions are highly routine and subject to fatigue. Any embellishments that are introduced in an effort to deal with emotional emptiness tend to become self-aggrandizing and to interfere with efficiency. An example of feminine productivity at an instinctual level is the nest building activity of birds. It utilizes techniques well adapted to the future function of the nest. Since the engineering skill of the bird is in no way experimental or subject to reason, any effort to add to the enjoyment of the task by willful alterations of technique could only lead to malfunction of the nest during the rearing period. Femininity cannot fulfill itself in its creative aspects in the familial functions. If it attempts the impossible, it expands

the familial feminine identity and thus compounds the
problem because the only pathway to a creative interpersonal
life lies in restricting the feminine social role to the irreducible minimum.

Unless power finds commitments in the world, it cannot
fulfill itself. The masculine social role as it is utilized for
the goals of family life cannot lead to a growing productive
interaction with the outside world. Within the family, the
individual must remain stable and reliable in his loyalties
and involvements. The meanings which power finds in
family life are elemental and expose the individual to
boredom. Any extraneous and creative interests which become focused within the family become outlets for egotistical
vanity and interfere with family cohesion. An example of
pure masculine expressiveness is the song of the male bird,
an activity which creates an atmosphere of unity in the
mated domain which is free from encroachment. The feeling
tone of the male bird is not based on an expanding sensitivity and it is not related to particular accomplishments.
He takes his mood of dominance for granted, and it is not
alloyed with self-consciousness. In this way he reaches a
maximum readiness to repel the challenge of other males to
his ownership of the domain. Masculinity cannot fulfill
itself in its creative aspects through intensifications of the
familial attachments. If it attempts to do so, it expands
the masculine social role at the expense of the autonomous
masculinity, and thus reduces the scope of the energies available for interaction with the outer world.

Among civilized human beings the masculine and feminine social identity goes only so far as is required by the
community standards which define it. The social identity is
like any other adaptive function. There is a basic minimum
psychological investment which the individual must find
if the automatic channels of social acceptance and cooperation are to be established. Any investment beyond this

point entraps the personality in an interpersonal world which leaves no room to utilize its inner growth potentials.

SOCIAL AND FAMILIAL ROLES

The social roles which express the surface masculine or feminine identity are stable, self-evident, and are based on highly communicable feelings and readily demonstrable modes of behavior. Such psychological resources cannot be put to work in dealing with the unknown and the chaotic. The individual in a state of growth invests a minimum of himself in his social role. A creative maturity is characterized by the ability to conform to a full adaptive social role without any encroachment on the inner identity.

An autonomous capacity for love seeks an involvement with others which taxes its capacity for understanding. The permanent nature of love requires a continuity of feeling which cannot be disrupted by the presence of problems. Love seeks a relationship with another person who needs love, but the sharing of love cannot be a simple flow between two people. Love must do psychological work to justify its existence. Without this autonomous capacity to maintain itself, love becomes the victim of any frustration which it meets, and as the capacity for love dies, the shrinkage of the inner self-awareness creates a crisis which can only be met by a helpless appeal for love from another.

An autonomous capacity for personal power seeks a commitment with others which takes the capacity for responsibility beyond its previous limits. The uncompromising nature of power requires a self-control which cannot be disrupted by the encountering of obstacles. Power seeks a relationship with another person who can make an alliance with it, but the sharing of a power interaction is not an automatic event. Power must develop new dimensions in its capacity for loyalty in order to justify its existence. This

autonomous capacity to expand into new areas where resources can be discovered and exploited confers on power
a self-generated integrity. Unless power is on this kind of
independent basis, it becomes the victim of any frustration
which it encounters, and as the capacity for a power attitude
dies, the shrinkage of self-confidence creates a crisis which
can only be met by an undisciplined attempt to win control
by arousing the sympathy and pity of another.

All men are required to establish masculine social roles,
and all women feminine ones. They bring these traits to
each other in their adaptive social intercourse, and the
contrast in their social identities provides a basic feminine
warmth and masculine pride which colors social interactions.
Society requires a minimal cohesiveness and readiness for
cooperation among its members, and this is facilitated by
gender differentiation, provided the differences are not
deepened and invigorated by inappropriate and intrusive
over-involvements.

The gender traits must be preserved in familial attachments but they can be shaped to individual needs by courtship activity. The courtship requires that the inner identity
expose itself. When both partners have the same yielding
or assertive identity, as they must have in a stable family
relationship, it becomes necessary for the basic character
to reveal itself as the real foundation of their attachment
and cooperation, and the contrast in the social roles fades
into the background of their personal life together.

FANTASY AND PLAY-ACTING

The psychological interactions between individuals which
serve the interests of psychological growth are private and
separate in relationship to the adaptive life of maturity.
If the individual is exclusively governed in his feelings and
attitudes by the established forms of his mature social roles,

there is no opportunity for the elaboration of fantasy and play-acting, which limits the development of new facets of sensitivity and initiative in human affairs. Enriching fantasy is only possible where the mind is free to explore feeling in any direction that brings a pleasurable self-awareness. Fantasy permits a maximum of selectivity in a world in which mobility is suspended. Once the individual has found new dimensions in himself in feeling, he is prepared to seek the necessary experiences which will permit the preliminary work of fantasy to lead him to a larger interaction with others. The individual does not act directly on his fantasies. He acts on the basis of the inner readiness for new experience which fantasy has created. Individuals who act out fantasies are ensnared by perverse mechanisms, and this is especially true in the sexual area. If the process replaces the adaptive life it becomes schizophrenic in nature.

Play-acting expands the scope of experience only where the individual is able to involve himself in any interest which brings enjoyable self-confidence. Play-acting permits a maximum mobility in a world in which selectivity of opportunity is suspended. Once the individual has expanded the scope of his capacities for entering experience, he is prepared to accept the necessary feeling attachments which will give a value to the preliminary work of play-acting. These commitments do not come directly out of play-acting itself. He accepts new feelingfulness out of the need for involvement that play-acting has created. Individuals who allow play-acting to usurp the place of a meaningful relationship with reality become the victims of addiction mechanisms, and this is especially true in the celebrative area. If the process spreads to the adaptive life it may become psychotic in proportion, leading to a manic-depressive type of disorganization.

Where fantasy is not free to follow channels of self-indulgent pleasure, there is not sufficient psychic investment to carry feelings into the areas where growth can occur. Because of the privacy of fantasy, it readily enters the sexuality of the individual. Yielding personalities who conform closely to the experiential patterns established by parental influence in childhood may develop an apparently rich fantasy life by taking over the fantasies of the parents. Such fantasy has no flexibility and is useless for independent growth. The conformity of the child is threatened at puberty by the emergence of sexuality since parental sexual fantasy is not communicated to the child. The adolescent must attempt to find sexual adequacy either through an autonomy he does not possess or through utilization of social roles which are inflexible in nature. His independent efforts often lead to the acting out of fantasies in a highly rebellious pattern. He ends with a loss of access to feelingfulness which may bring catastrophic depressive reactions with suicidal consequences.

Where play-acting cannot find autonomous and egocentric enjoyment, there is not sufficient psychic investment to develop new modalities of self-expression. Because of the dissociated quality of play-acting, it readily enters the celebrative area. Assertive personalities who submit completely to familial patterns of feeling may develop an apparently resourceful capacity for play by taking over the parental modes of self-expression in this area. Such play is not flexible and cannot establish a basis for independent growth. The conformity of the growing child is threatened at puberty by the emergence of the celebrative capacities, since parental celebrative experiences are not shared with the child. The adolescent must explore celebration with an autonomy he does not possess or confine himself to identification with the patterns of the established social roles. His independent efforts often lead to overwhelming involvements in evanescent thrill-seeking undertakings. If he chooses dependence on the conventional roles to which he has access, he must accept a rigidity which is beyond alteration by himself. This deprivation leads to a premature maturity which undermines the capacity for mood elevation, leading to a heretical and irresponsible exposure to self-destruction.

SHAME AND GUILT

The feeling of inferiority arises from an inability to enter experience on a scope which can provide an outlet for the feeling resources of the individual. It is the fundamental psychic motivation which leads the yielding personality to expand its awareness of the world. The feeling of shame cannot be overcome by mere activity, but only through that kind of self-development which carries within it new modalities of experience. The more the individual understands, the more avenues of self-expression open to him. In this way he preserves the sensitive orientation of his inner identity while developing a full commitment to a life of organization for action. Fantasy plays a substantial role in guiding the direction of his self-development. The most pleasurable self-awareness comes from that kind of inner identity which provides him with unobstructed channels of constructive action. The kind of mastery sought by the yielding personality comes as a gift from the hands of insight.

The sense of guilt arises when feelingfulness cannot find the depth which permits commitment to meaningful patterns of action. It is the fundamental psychic motivation which leads the assertive personality to expand its scope of interaction with others. The sense of guilt cannot be overcome by sentimental feeling which is its own reason for being, but only through that kind of loyalty which brings new avenues of sensitivity in human interaction. The wider the scope of the interpersonal responsibilities, the more meaning develops in the individual life. In this way a man preserves the spontaneity of his inner self while finding a lasting commitment to a life which is oriented by feeling. Play-acting guides the development of his expanding interpersonal responsibilities. The most enjoyable self-confidence comes from that kind of inner identity which provides him with uncomplicated access to meaningful loyalties unalloyed by doubt. The kind of insight sought by the assertive personality comes to him as the by-product of mastery.

Where the growing child is too strongly influenced by the parental fantasies, there is not an adequate opportunity for the finding of new experience. Whatever independent enrichment of the inner self the child is able to attain remains locked within himself because of the degree of his attachment to the parental image of his social and familial roles. Such states of feelingfulness lead to a growing inner awareness which is burdened with self-conscious shame. When sexuality emerges at puberty, there is a sudden and often catastrophic increase in the kind of self-awareness which cannot find access to the world.

Where the patterns of play-acting are taken over from the parents, there is no opportunity for the exploration of new areas of involvement. Whatever independent elaboration of spontaneity the growing child can establish remains in an unavowed dissociated area, banished from interaction with others, due to the exclusive commitment to the conventional masculine image of the parents. Such states of readiness for action lead to an expanding inner self-confidence which has no outlet and is burdened with guilt. When the celebrative capacities emerge at puberty, there is a sudden and disorganizing increase in the level of the kind of personal self-confidence which cannot find a real world in which to fulfill itself.

CREATIVITY AND THE SURPLUSES

The inner character of man can only find creative outlets in interpersonal relationships when the sexual and celebrative surpluses are not used to form a domain. The creative spirit can thrive only when love can reach the greatest depths without necessarily becoming sexualized, and power can extend without predetermined limits without inevitable overflow into the celebrative state. The work of love is the only ultimate antidote to the sense of inferiority, and the loyalties of power alone can bring the sense of meaning which can resolve guilt. It is sexual fantasy which brings the greatest shame, and celebrative play-acting which accumulates the greatest guilt. Because the familial functions provide a place for sex and celebration, they tend to relieve shame and guilt through the social acceptance which accompanies family life. The surpluses which are expressed within the conventional patterns of married life put shame and guilt outside the scope of individual accountability, thus diluting them and nullifying their individual impact.

The capacity to handle shame and guilt independently is an essential element in establishing a creative relationship with the world. Love cannot deepen without dealing with the sexual tendencies which are inevitably aroused in the process, nor can power expand its scope in human affairs without dealing with the celebrative components that are stirred by it. An individual who cannot deal with his own sexual and celebrative tendencies autonomously must invest so much of himself in his familial involvements as to make significant participation in creative interpersonal activity impossible. Family life, in spite of the place it makes for the surpluses, is still part of the basic adaptive life of mankind.

There is no such thing as a significant increase in the depth of the yielding personality which does not bring a new influx of sexual responsiveness. This sexual increment tends to follow a mated pattern and is not readily confined to the established familial patterns of expression. Since the core of the yielding personality is feminine, the individual must deal with an awareness of sexual responsiveness to surplus masculinity in the world. Any significant increase in the vigor of the assertive personality brings a new influx of celebrative tendencies. This celebrative increment tends to follow a mated pattern, breaking away from the established familial channels of expression. Since the core of the assertive personality is masculine, the individual must deal with a strong self-confident readiness to possess any feminine elements in the world that are open to exploitation.

Mated tendencies which deepen and invigorate the idealizing and constructive capacities tend to alter the adaptive social life, bringing withdrawal and indifference into familial interactions. This creates the psychological atmosphere of adolescence. If the tendency to invest the surpluses in a mated pattern are overcome, the new sexual and celebrative components remain as unattached elements in the personality, seeking outlet where they can. They find a private and separate existence which can be made harmonious with the adaptive requirements of living. There is so much of unconventional sex and celebration within the fabric of civilized living that this state of affairs can be taken to be part of normal human psychology. Men accept the obligation of protecting the secret and separate status of these phenomena. As long as a substantial part of sexual feeling and behavior is hidden, honest communication about man's sexual life remains difficult, and sexual problems are left to the individual to deal with as he can. As long as the celebrative attitudes and involvements remain in an unavowed dissociated state, the individual is deprived of the cooperation he may need in dealing with these tendencies.

REPRESSION AND RENUNCIATION

Since sex and celebration are not fully channeled into conventional familial outlets, they tend to establish their own patterns of expression, using those human relationships which lie outside adaptive involvements. The diversity of these forms can be very great, and their variety is a clear indication that the mated domain which is found in nature is not operating in the psychological life of civilized human beings.

Deviations in the patterns of sexual expression take their origin in the need to overcome discontent in sexual experience. Man accepts the psychological task of building and elaborating his sexual capacities on his own. Without adequate sexual gratification man remains in an unremitting search for it. Dissatisfaction in this area remains a challenge which preoccupies him and leads to inner efforts toward new orientation in his feeling with others. Adequate sexuality depends both on an involvement in sexual sensuality and a capacity for orgastic discharge.

Celebrative enjoyment is also subject to variations in the patterns of expression, and the restless search for celebrative adequacy is motivated by a lack of spontaneity in this area. Man seeks celebrative self-abandonment because this psychological state is an essential aspect of inner freedom. When it is obstructed the individual searches for it in a restless fashion, leading to efforts to make a new organization of his energies in relationship to others. Adequate celebration depends both on a vigor of the celebrative mood and a capacity for inner surrender to the circumstances which release the sense of freedom.

The search for sexual and celebrative fulfillment parallels a growth in the inner identity. If the feminine core of the yielding personality is a threat to the masculine social role of the individual, he may reject those kinds of interpersonal interactions which bring awareness of his psychological femininity. Under these conditions the masculine social role is preserved at the cost of psychological independence since flexibility and growth can only occur when the yielding personality has sufficient inner security to find new insights. The privacy which takes its being in the sustaining of aloneness becomes alien to his psychological balance. His identity becomes attached to the kind of masculine experience which can only be found through dependence on socially established avenues of action. Whatever sexual adequacy comes with this state of balance he must accept without dissatisfaction, and under these circumstances he learns not to question his sexual adjustment. To be aware of discontent means to threaten the whole basis of his masculine social adequacy. Feelings which are foreign to his pattern of adjustment lose access to self-awareness, and sexuality which does not serve his masculine social role is seen as deviant and pathological. The search for sexual fulfillment is cut off, and sexual control is elevated to the status of a primary aspect of maturity. Self-control is only possible where it receives a wide social support. The sexuality which does not fit the social role is seen as shameful, and if such feelings do not emerge because of the avoidance of the experiences which could bring them to self-awareness, the individual may lose access to knowledge of them. This process is called repression, although there is no actual repressing force at work. In the presence of such repression self-control is no longer necessary.

If the masculine core of the assertive personality becomes a threat to the capacity for social conformity, the individual may turn away from those interpersonal involvements which bring the masculine self-confidence into focus. Under these conditions, the balance of the personality is preserved at the cost of psychological independence since autonomous growth can only occur when the assertive personality has sufficient freedom to find new avenues of mastery. The separateness which takes its being in the capacity to lay aside established commitments cannot operate where it is alien to psychological balance. The individual becomes imprisoned by the kind of feminine access to feeling which can only be found by dependence on socially shared beliefs. Whatever celebrative adequacy comes with this state of balance he must accept without dissatisfaction and he learns not to expose himself to the alternatives. To be aware of unhappiness means to threaten the whole basis of the feminine elements of his social attainments. Attitudes which are foreign to his pattern of adjustment are no longer used to reach self-confidence, and celebrative patterns which do not conform to his social role are seen as deviant and antisocial. The search for celebrative spontaneity is blocked, and celebrative discipline becomes an essential part of social maturity. This kind of discipline is only possible where it receives broad social reinforcement. The celebrative impulses which are seen as non-conforming are experienced only with guilt, and as they disappear from the personality through avoidance of the situations which tend to evoke them, the individual is no longer called upon to deal with them in any way. This is the process of renunciation, which is the experiential equivalent of repression. In the presence of renunciation, discipline is no longer necessary.

PSYCHOLOGICAL INDEPENDENCE
AND THE SURPLUSES

The masculine social role can be fulfilled by adherence to socially established traits which the community recognizes as masculine, without regard to the inner identity. Individuals with a feminine inner identity have a tendency toward excessive privacy in their psychic life, as a consequence of their need to establish their social role. In the case of individuals with a masculine inner identity, the masculine social role is easier to establish, but the tendency to invest the whole self in this role brings disappointment and frustration to a degree which forces the individual to an excessive dissociation of his energies.

Unless the private and secret aspects of love become a bridge to experience for the individual, the sensitivity and feelingfulness of the inner self remains walled off from the world of interaction with others. This is especially evident in the area of sexual fantasy. The individual does not employ all the depth he has in adaptive relationships with others, and if his full capacity for depth of feeling is never brought into the light of day, his faith in the meaning of love in human affairs ceases to function in a creative fashion. Where there is a tyrannical spread of the adaptive functions, the love orientation ceases to find access to self-awareness, and a process of forgetting effaces the consciousness of this aspect of the self. There is a difference between privacy and absence of self-knowledge. The deepest part of the self can exist and grow only in the secure world which the secret inner life creates, but this security can never be a stable one. Under the pressure of the sense of inferiority there is an unrelenting reaching toward putting love to work in human affairs, and love which operates without self-knowledge and unabashed honesty finds itself deprived of the essence of its identity.

Unless the separate and dissociated aspect of personal power becomes an avenue to feelingful awareness, the vigor and spontaneity of the inner self cannot find genuine attachments. This is especially true in the area of celebrative play. The individual cannot use all of the vigor of which he is capable in his adaptive relationships, and if his entire potential for participation in experience is never actually utilized in interpersonal relationships, the anticipation of growth and development which hope alone can sustain must be put aside. When there is a dogmatic ensnarement of the adaptive energies in socially rigid patterns, the power drives cease to find expression in a growing self-confidence, and a process of resignation effaces all manifestations of this aspect of the self. Dissociation of action patterns does not mean loss of the sense of participation in these separate experiences since that which is dissociated is capable of expression under conditions of freedom from restraint. The most spontaneous part of the self can exist and grow only in that world of psychological freedom which the separate inner life creates, but access to this atmosphere of freedom is never an established fact of life in the sense that adaptive patterns are. Under the pressure of the sense of guilt there is an unrelenting inner need to find human resources which provide an outlet for personal power, and power which tries to establish itself without courageous innovation finds itself deprived of the essence of its constructive identity.

The capacity for privacy in psychological life leads to autonomy in the personality, but only when inner secrecy does not lead to a loss of self-knowledge. The capacity to sustain access to spontaneous action, dissociated from established social values, leads to inner autonomy, but only when such activity is not characterized by loss of self-investment in the dissociated behavior. Man's great capacity for privacy leads to elaborations of fantasy, and sexuality readily flows into this area. Awareness of his own sexuality is an essential part of self-knowledge, and masturbatory phenomena are released in the process. Man's access to spontaneous dissociated patterns of behavior leads to elaborations of play, and celebrative tendencies flow readily into such activity. The ability to deal with his celebrative nature is an essential part of self-control, and a readiness for thrill seeking enjoyment is released in the process.

CREATIVITY AND MATURITY

The adaptive interactions which make up maturity and bring the social roles into being leave a place for the creative surpluses of civilized man, but they cannot directly guide and support them. If maturity is tyrannical and dogmatic in its utilization of psychological resources, there will be an emptiness of affect and a depression of mood that only becomes an increasing burden as the commitments to adaptive involvements grow in scope. Expanding investment in adaptive activities becomes parasitic on the inner psychological life. The scope of adaptive life can and must develop if the maturity of the individual is to maintain social adequacy in a changing world, but if the individual is in an active phase of creative personal growth, expansion of the adaptive life is difficult or impossible.

Where men react against depressive tendencies by seeking to invest more of themselves in their adaptive life, they tend to distort the nature of the world around them. They attempt to idealize the traits of others which further their own adaptive development, rather than idealizing psychological qualities which have universal meaning. They search for responsiveness in others on the basis of preconceptions which are fixed by their social commitments, rather than on a basis of exploring the actual resources which are inherent in human nature. They see the world through the eyes of their own ambitious strivings and deal with the world as an exercise in promoting social acceptance.

Where worldly ambition becomes the channel of self-development, rather than the inner growth which comes from the work of love, the ideal being served becomes false, and idealism becomes the servant of self-aggrandizing tendencies. Such idealism actually serves the power tendencies of the self. The individual's adaptive aspirations make up the substance of his ideal. Truth seeking in such circumstances must stop when insights have attained usefulness in adaptive ways, and they have no necessary relationship to the abiding truth which exists for its own sake.

Where the need for an increasing social acceptance becomes the channel of self-development, rather than the inner growth which comes from the explorations of personal power, the search for reality loses its responsible qualities and reality becomes a tool of personal vanity. The individual guides his behavior by the response he gains from others, without regard to his personal integrity. He accepts those loyalties which prove useful to him, and interpersonal reality becomes a reflection of his own nature. The development of mastery in such circumstances ends with adaptive accomplishment, and there is no necessary relationship with the kind of uncompromising right which has an existence of its own.

THE INDIVIDUAL AND SOCIAL PROGRESS

Human understanding can remain in the service of love, or it can become a means of power seeking. When truth exists for its own sake, its insights are an entity which has an existence of its own. These insights become a resource for others to use, either in the search for more truth, or as a resource in the hands of those individuals who are capable of the creative expansion of the right. Truth can set men free, but the thinker himself is not the agent of this release from bondage. Society must have both thinkers and men of action if it is to fulfill the creative potentials that are inherent in truth and right, and their interaction is essential to social progress.

The expanding capacity for responsibility which comes from personal power can remain a goal in itself, seeking always new human resources, or it can become the means of self-idealization. When the right exists for its own sake, its modalities of mastery become an entity which attracts the identification of others. They may use these modes of behavior in establishing new mastery, or their embodiment of moral integrity may provide an ideal for those who do the creative work of love. The right can make men secure, but the man of action is not in a position to make this security a source of creative productivity for himself.

All the insights and modalities of mastery which human beings develop in their interpersonal life are potentially available for use in practical adaptive activities. This kind of application of truth and right can only come when circumstances make fruitful utilization possible. Truth and right may lie fallow in human affairs for years, decades, or centuries, depending on the course of social progress and the lack of access to the social problems and obstacles to which they could be applied. When men turn away from creative productivity because of the lack of avenues for practical application, their capacity for inner growth disappears. Creativity is a personal accomplishment, and the social gain which accrues from it must depend on factors which lie outside the control of any given individual.

There can be no guarantee of social progress out of the creative contributions of any individual thinker or builder. It is the process of making the contribution itself, and the personal life of access to growth which goes with it, that provides the reward for the creative mode of living. The autonomy which interpersonal creativity requires must be paid for in the rejection of easy access to communication of ideas and to ready demonstrability of modes of control. If the individual does not find his own way in interpersonal relationships, sustaining the aloneness and separateness which such independence brings, he cannot use his own life for the exploration of the meaning of new experience and the value of new concepts. The intellectual enters new experience only when his autonomous capacity to explore meanings remains intact. The man of action exposes himself to new concepts only when his autonomous capacity to develop moral values remains intact. Self-awareness and self-confidence are the basic tools of a creative interpersonal life.

AGGRESSION AND PASSIVITY

Civilized man has a surplus of insights and modalities of mastery which has no necessary or inevitable application to the practical affairs of every day life. The existence of this surplus is taken for granted in the impersonal fields of physical science and engineering. When men accumulate insights and mastery in human affairs, the tendency to apply them to their adaptive social life may become irresistible. Men live in a world of expanding psychological needs and purposes, and this developmental tendency may lead to a compulsive need to gain material and self-aggrandizing adaptive rewards, or to an obsessive involvement in purposes which gratify adaptive egotism. Any increment in the psychological striving toward material success or popular acceptance tends to weaken the inner commitment to creative goals. When access to conventional success is difficult, inner growth is often facilitated, and conversely, men can lose their devotion to higher purposes when the broad and open road to worldly advantage lies unobstructed before them.

When men withhold themselves from an overinvolvement with the practical and adaptive social interactions, they utilize the mechanisms of withdrawal and indifference. The establishment of a boundary between the creative and the adaptive is a difficult psychological task. The price for living a truth seeking life has often been the acceptance of a priest-like retreat, and men who wish to establish the right may find themselves in a soldier's enlistment. If men put too much of themselves into the day to day involvements of practical living, they find that they are using big tools for little tasks. Love cannot do its work where these is nothing worthy of being loved, nor can power find attachments where there is no genuine opportunity for its kind of integrity. A personality which is both mature and creative is capable of great flexibility in its investment in the adaptive aspect of living. It expands only where circumstances so dictate, and never as a means of inner self-fulfillment. Even though the stresses of life circumstances may call for a major increase in the investment in adaptive interactions, a part of the self remains above and beyond practical affairs, ready to find its proper sphere of expression when opportunity presents itself. Although man is thus a victim of circumstance, the core of his personality remains uncommitted save in areas of his own choosing.

Where there is a fixed commitment to the utilization of all the resources of the inner self in the adaptive social life, the compulsive and obsessive mechanisms come into play. The yielding personality cannot any longer seek truth as an end in itself, but only in terms of its utilization for adaptive ends. The inner feminine core of the personality has none of the security which selective withdrawal confers, and faith no longer has any meaning. Driven by the compulsive need for adaptive success, truth loses its independent identity and becomes the victim of power manipulations. If these power activities are to reach socially successful channels of expression, they need to be shared and reinforced by others, since they can never attain a genuine creative autonomy. This kind of power organization exploits weaknesses in others and does not bring new resources into existence. It flows into areas where there is no effective resistance, justifying itself by a self-serving moral code, and maintains itself by the mutual idealization of similar personalities. The power that builds nothing but the personal advantage of the individual is called aggression. Although aggression serves the individual's adaptive goals rather than the interests of society, it can only exist successfully where it receives social support.

The mechanism of passivity comes into operation when personal power is unable to resist being captured by the adaptive life. The assertive personality loses its freedom to reach for the right as an end in itself. The inner masculine core of the personality requires the mobility which indifference makes possible. Without a genuine mobility, hopefulness cannot translate itself into experiences which make a significant difference. The individual becomes the prisoner of his own loyalties. The right loses its independent identity and is undermined by a parasitic need for love. If these love attachments are to have an adaptive meaning, they must be shared and reinforced by others since they can never attain a creative autonomy. This kind of love orientation submits to the vanity of others and cannot bring new ideals into existence. It is readily captured by surface emotionality and pretense, establishing an aura of permanence through the sharing of cultistic beliefs, and maintains itself by mutual exploitation among similar personalities. The kind of automatic love that understands nothing except the need of another for unquestioning acceptance underlies the passive mechanism, and it cannot exist without social reinforcement.

THE PSYCHOLOGICAL CONTENT
OF INTERPERSONAL CREATIVITY

Man can only fulfill himself as a creative human being by withholding himself from a full commitment to the demands of adaptive social living. To succeed in this psychological task requires constant flexibility in assessing the minimum basic requirements of mature social conformity.

He skirts the edge of rebellion and heresy in his unconventional self and risks a loss of inner identity in his adaptive roles.

Individuals who maintain a clear inner identity must
find the psychological security and freedom which are essential to its existence. If the individual is committed to
patterns of maturity which leave no room for independent
growth, a conflict must occur which renders the inner self
alien to the world of maturity. This conflict may take up
so much of the psychic life as to threaten the capacity for
adaptive living.

 A yielding personality has more need of love than his
mature social interactions can use. An assertive personality
has more personal power to express than his adaptive social
world can absorb. These creative reservoirs of tension and
energy must find an interaction with the human world
that lies above and beyond the adaptive demands. The
creative interface between man and his human world involves itself with the personal contentment and happiness
of other people. Genuine creative attachments between individuals must be concerned with the psychological fundamentals which society as a whole cannot reach. Such
attachments keep growth capacity open by reaching a communication and a readiness for cooperation which are based
on honest mutual exposure and unqualified helpfulness
which is not obstructed by social cowardice. Creative love
is a personal feeling which will not disappear in the presence of problems, and creative power is a personal attitude
which will not compromise when it encounters obstacles.

When men interact for the purpose of making a better
life for each other, love has a meaning which permits
an unlimited depth without inevitable sexualization, and
power has a value which guides it into an ever-expanding
scope without a necessary celebrative overflow. The unlimited feelingfulness on which love is based must ulti-

mately accept awareness of the sexuality in others. Taking
cognizance of sexuality creates a psychological stress in the
creative individual who carries unattached sexuality within
himself because the empathetic reinforcement of sexuality
must not be allowed to destroy the basis on which love
does its work. When the unattached sexuality leads to a
direct response to the sexuality of others, it becomes intrusive on the creative aspect of interpersonal relationships.
Civilized man makes a place for his sexuality, and in all
other aspects of his psychological life he avoids sexualization,
not by rejecting the deep tension bearing capacities of his
personality, but by utilizing these tensions for creative
purposes.

The untrammeled spontaneity which gives rise to personal power does not allow itself to overflow automatically
into celebrative experiences, but it must ultimately include
the celebrative nature of others in the world of its social
control. Interacting with the celebrative nature of others
creates a stress in the creative individual who carries within
himself an unattached celebrative surplus, since he must
not allow his own celebrative attitudes to obliterate his
awareness of the subtleties of his world of opportunity.
When the unattached celebrative tendencies draw the individual into an identification with the celebrative behavior
of others without choice on his part, it undermines the
creative aspect of interpersonal relationships. Civilized man
makes an established place for his celebrative needs. In the
creative aspects of his psychological life he bypasses his
celebrative tendencies, not by rejecting his spontaneity, but
by using his energy reserve for creative purposes.

THE MECHANISMS OF AGGRESSION
AND PASSIVITY

When the capacity for an expanding comprehension of

the environment is committed to the adaptive goals of the individual, insights are directly translated into practical mastery. Such power strivings are guided entirely by their social effectiveness and remain relatively free of celebrative components. The power goals take form only when accomplishment is assured. The tools of mastery are assets which dictate the direction power takes. Aggressive power has no value unless it is effective in advancing the interests of the individual, since the building of mastery is not a goal in itself. Aggression flows into the channels where resistance is ineffective. If aggression can convince others that it is right, it can exploit their submissive tendencies to enlarge the scope of its opportunities. The primary tool of aggression is the control of the minds of other men. It operates by usurping the place of the masculine ideal in civilized social life. This is a complex psychological undertaking which requires community support to be effective. Aggressive power can often outweigh the power that is inherent in the right because it does not need to be concerned with the enrichment of the whole of society with new resources. If aggression builds, it is only because its immediate goals can be served in this fashion, and destruction can become equally acceptable. Aggression utilizes emergency mechanisms because its survival is always at stake. Resistance to its will is met with anger and where victory is likely, a readiness for a fight reaction. There is no basic security or peace of mind which can be conferred by the aggressive mechanism. If it does not continue to spread its influence, it is vulnerable to exposure by genuine truth and an ensuing collapse of its effectiveness.

When the capacity for an expanding manipulative ability is committed to the adaptive goals of the individual, mastery accepts confinement by practical rules. The love attachments of the individual are formed through the adherence to socially useful feelings and remain relatively free of sexualization. Loyalties flow in the channels where a mutual reinforcement of these feelings is assured. Love operates in areas defined by socially established patterns of mutual understanding. Passive love has no meaning unless it expands interpersonal cohesion without conceptual effort since the development of insights is not a goal in itself. Passivity is at home where feelings are characteristically exposed and dramatized as a means of heightening the feeling level of a group. If passivity can usurp the place of truth, it can attract the loyalties of others for the purpose of controlling their behavior. The essence of passive love lies in its capacity to entrap others into automatic commitments to action. It operates by usurping the place of the reality of feminine responsiveness in civilized social life. This is a complex psychological process which requires community reinforcement for its establishment. Passive love is often more effective in appealing to men's responsiveness than the love that serves truth because it does not need to be concerned with the revelation of the genuine ideals which have validity for the whole of society. If passivity expands understanding it is only because its immediate needs can be served in this way, and falsehood which is readily believed is equally acceptable. Passivity utilizes emergency mechanisms because its existence is always at stake. Rejection of its beliefs and loyalties is met with hate and a readiness for withdrawal by means of a flight reaction. There is no genuine freedom which can come out of the passive mechanism. If it does not continue to gain adherents, it will be destroyed by the emergence of the right because it will lose its capacity to establish automatic social empathy.

The aggressive mechanism rests on a cynical use of human cohesion. The aggressive distortion of the masculine ideal attracts submissive love from others for the purpose of enlarging the social power role, and individual creative power is ignored or depreciated. The passive mechanism rests on an opportunistic use of human cooperation. The passive distortion of the feminine responsive capacities arouses dominant power attitudes in others for the purpose of exploiting their capacity for helpfulness. This need for expansion of social ties and identifications is guided by the social advantages obtained, and individual creative love loses its meaning.

Because personal power is not important in an aggressive world, the difficulties associated with the creative struggles of personal power, especially the tendency toward an over-flow of energies into celebrative channels, are more readily avoided. Aggressive power has all the outward qualities of social maturity and it is only when circumstances reveal the hidden defects in the love orientation of the aggressive individual that the perverse structure of the personality stands revealed. Because autonomous love is not important in a world which exploits passivity, the difficulties associated with the search for creative love, especially the tendency toward the sexualization of love ties, are more readily avoided. Passive love has an apparently mature social iden-tity, and it is only when circumstances expose the moral defects which accompany passive social conformity that the addicted distortions of the personality stand revealed.

PHOBIC AND PSYCHOPATHIC MECHANISMS

The yielding personality is dependent on the social role for access to experience in the mature aspect of interpersonal relationships. If the masculine identity which comes from the social role is too rigidly organized because of aggressive contamination, the individual may have difficulty in accept-ing his mature status. There is an ensuing inhibition at the level of finding new experience. If the individual seeks mental health through rebellion, he may fail to elaborate a genuine masculine ideal and will remain fixed in a hateful relationship to aggressive authoritarian figures in his psychological world. If he attempts to cast his inhibitions aside, he will find himself flooded by his own aggressive tendencies. The creative pathway for meeting this problem requires a withdrawal from the psychological involvement with false ideals. Such a withdrawal leaves the individual with a surplus of feeling which is unattached, and this surplus is vulnerable to sexualization. There is an inherent danger of loss of a meaningful relationship to others in this kind of withdrawal, and the rising quantity of unattached feelingfulness may be perceived as a threat to psychic equilibrium with resultant anxiety. The individual becomes vulnerable to sudden increases of disorienting anxiety whenever the environment ceases to provide familiar guide lines to patterns of behavior. Inner panic in the face of the new and unfamiliar is called phobic anxiety.

The assertive personality is dependent on the social role for access to cohesive feeling in the mature aspect of interpersonal relationships. If the feminine influences which come from this source are excessively dogmatic because of passive orientation, the individual may turn away from mature social commitments. There is an ensuing perplexity at the level of finding new awareness in interpersonal relationships. If the individual seeks social conformity through a cultistic attachment to a deviant fraction of the community, he will not be able to develop his capacities for dealing with a genuinely responsive reality and will remain fixed in an angry and provocative relationship with the passive law-giving elements of his psychological world. If he attempts to accept his passive nature, taking his perplexity for granted, he will become lost in his own accumulating social helplessness. The creative pathway for dealing with the parasitic aspect of passive love requires an indifference to the temptations inherent in its surface attractiveness and shallow promises. Such an attitude of indifference leaves the individual with a surplus potential for involvement in experience, and this surplus is vulnerable to celebrative expression. Indifference of this kind threatens the capacity to establish interpersonal relationships of enduring value, and a rising quantity of uncommitted energies may create a state of disagreeable detachment with pathological restlessness. The individual becomes vulnerable to sudden increases of disorganizing mobile tendencies whenever the environment fails to keep reliable channels of submission open. Impulsive and restless behavior which defies self-control in the face of what is new and not understood in the responses of others constitutes the psychopathic mechanism.

If the individual exposes himself to the unfamiliar but rejects adaptive involvement with it, his awareness of the environment is fragmented and his orientation fails. He enters experience enshrouded in a sense of security which is inappropriate to the circumstances. His self-awareness does not lead out into the world, yet he is involved in activities which require orientation. The external world stimulates him but he cannot relate himself to it. The rising level of dissonant self-awareness brings anxiety, and if the inner distress reaches the breaking point, he must withdraw from relationship with the unfamiliar. The point at which mobility breaks down is the phobic barrier. The phobic state creates boundaries which limit mobility to the areas where orientation can be assured without psychic work.

If the individual becomes involved with potential opportunities which prove resistive to his will and yet make no place for adaptive interaction, his self-confidence fails to maintain continuity and his organization for integrated action fails. He accepts involvements in a dissociated way, maintaining a freedom which is inappropriate to the circumstances. His self-confidence cannot reach the outer world in a meaningful way, yet he needs the organization which goal directed behavior can bring. The external world invites his participation, but he cannot find a consistent relationship. The rising level of dissociated self-confidence which ensues is perceived as dangerous and leads to uncontrolled restlessness. If the inner disharmony becomes too great, he must cease to feel with his provocative environment and indifference takes over, leading to a broad detachment from all loyalties. At this point he is no longer called upon to make discriminations and his submissive tendencies disappear. This breakdown in selectivity is the psychopathic release. The psychopathic state makes room for selectivity only in areas where inner organization is assured without psychic work.

REBELLION AND HERESY

Neurosis and delinquency are the consequences of a refusal to accept maturity. If the individual is overwhelmed by neurotic or delinquent tendencies he remains dependent in a familial pattern, and his interaction with the world becomes emptied of creative psychological content, being dissipated in hate and anger reactions. The personality relates itself to the outer world as if it were capable of a creative interaction with it, but it cannot maintain the mobility and selectivity which independent psychological growth requires. The psychic struggle contained within neurosis and delinquency is directed toward the reinforcement of an emerging creative inner identity in the face of intimidating and seductive forces contained within a tyrannical and dogmatic maturity. If the individual succeeds in bringing this struggle to a favorable conclusion, he elaborates sufficient maturity to meet the minimum adaptive requirements of his community while preserving a maximum commitment to the creative aspect of his interpersonal relationships. If he cannot find the psychological resources for the slow growth process which this undertaking requires, it is possible for the individual to turn toward the espousal of aggressive power and passive love, through the use of conventional social supports. This is a process of finding psychological health and social harmony by a direct route, acting in the name of mature social behavior, but it carries within its adaptive rewards the ultimate threat of an emergence of serious affective emptiness and depression of mood.

Neurosis and delinquency maintain an unstable equilibrium within the personality for longer or shorter periods. The refusal of the neurotic to become mature is based on a rebellion against immorality. He cannot find truth out of his own resources, and he refuses to act on any other basis in those areas where his surplus capacities are involved. The neurotic cannot find growth through faith. Instead, he stands still through inhibition, utilizing patience to maintain equilibrium. When the delinquent turns away from mature goals, it is because he has become heretical toward established principles which he finds dishonest and superficial. He cannot find the right out of his own resources, and he will not accept loyalties which do not arise from involvement with the right in any area where his surplus capacities are being utilized. The delinquent cannot find growth through the influence of hope. Instead, he finds himself in a state of chronic perplexity, using endurance to keep inner balance.

The neurotic rebellion is against authority which is derived from the family and its extensions in the community. Outside the family circle the idealizing tendencies tend to focus on institutionalized authority, especially in the political realm. Submissiveness to social institutions gives access to action in dependent ways, and any break in this dependent tie has revolutionary implications. The heresy of the delinquent rejects the principles which come from the influence of the family and its extensions in the community. Beyond the scope of family beliefs he searches in the realm of socially supported ideas for truth which is safe from doubt. The repository of this view of the world is to be found in religion. The sense of self-fulfillment which comes from his exploitation of religious ideas gives access to loyalty in dependent ways, and if there is a dissolution of this devotion, the individual is drawn into mystical and cultistic philosophical preoccupations in which social communication is limited to fellow believers.

COMPULSIVE AND OBSESSIVE MECHANISMS

The compulsive mechanism comes into play when the neurotic personality accepts the limited world of his phobic encirclement as if it were complete, thereby bringing the awareness of an ideal to an end. The surplus in feeling within the individual is drained off by dutiful elaboration of functions arising from the social role. The compulsive individual has accepted an imprisonment of which he is no longer aware. If he is not to be emptied of feeling in his world of rigid boundaries, he must continue to serve truth with an expanding psychic investment, but the truth itself cannot grow. He becomes endlessly selective and discriminatory in patterns which are adaptive and mature in structure, but betray their neurotic source in the inappropriate surplus of feeling with which they are invested. The compulsive mechanism spares the individual from the struggle over the sexualization of his feeling surpluses, and in this way he avoids phobic anxiety. There is a resultant adaptive efficiency which is elaborated for its own sake, but the adaptation cannot find goals worthy of its expansionist tendencies.

The obsessive mechanism invades the personality threatened by psychopathic tendencies when the individual accepts the limited world of his superficial attachments as if it em-

bodied permanence. This mechanism brings the search for
a more responsive reality to an end. The surplus energy
outlets are captured by established needs and desires arising
from the social role. The individual who is guided by obsessive feelings has accepted a release from expanding depth
of involvement with others without realizing that he has
lost control of his own destiny. If his self-confident mood is
not to be undermined in his world of surface relationships,
he must continue to identify himself with the right with an
expanding energy investment, but his autonomous capacity
for finding the right cannot grow. He becomes superficially
mobile and manipulative in patterns which are adaptive and
mature in structure, but they betray their delinquent source
in the inappropriate surplus of energy with which they are
invested. The obsessive mechanism spares the individual
from the struggle against the celebrative channeling of his
surplus energies and thus avoids psychopathic restlessness.
There is a resultant adaptive harmony to which he clings for
its own sake, but the adaptation cannot find a world of opportunity which is worthy of its expansionist tendencies.

The compulsive individual bypasses the immorality inherent in aggression. His personal power outlets are channeled by a need for mastery which is confined within rigid
boundaries, and as long as he remains within these limits he
feels secure. The deeper tensions are not allowed to mount,
being repeatedly discharged out of inner need and not in
relationship to an expanding awareness of the outside world.
Compulsive power manipulations expend themselves without altering anything except the inner psychic life of the
individual. The emergency nature of the mechanism for
tension discharge is accepted as a characteristic of normal
living. The maintenance of a stable equilibrium exacts the
price of a constant readiness for compulsive self-expression.
The most significant of compulsive mechanisms is to be

found in compulsive thinking. In this area there is a maximum of manipulative structure with a minimum of interaction with others. The apparent pleasure which comes from compulsive thinking is not genuine, but seems to be there because of the temporary reassurance and relief from painful tension which it brings.

The individual whose personality is dominated by obsessive feeling is not aware of this mechanism since the essence of the process is contained in the sense of inevitability which characterizes it. Obsessive personalities avoid the espousal of ignorance and the accompanying resignation to fate which is inherent in passivity. The individual finds personal love outlets which are allowed to flow only in prescribed channels, and as long as he confines his interpersonal loyalties to these areas he maintains a sense of freedom. The larger energy accumulations are discharged before they become disturbing to the equilibrium, out of inner need and not in relationship to an expanding self-confidence directed toward the outer world. Obsessive love attachments find their own meanings, and the ultimate test of their apparent truth lies in their usefulness in preventing a rising energy from threatening the personality. Obsessive love operates as an emergency mechanism which is not itself subject to insight, and the price of social conformity is paid in a constant readiness for obsessive self-awareness. The most significant of obsessive mechanisms is found in the surrender to elemental and automatic feeling states in which the individual is drawn into patterns of behavior which he does not control. In this area there is a maximum of awareness of sensuality with a minimum of analytic and problem solving thought. The sense of pseudo-freedom which comes from obsessively channeled avenues of behavior looms large because of the apparent enjoyment accompanying the release of energy accumulations.

ANALYTIC THINKING AND
INVENTIVE MANIPULATION

The compulsive and obsessive mechanisms are often paired together in psychiatric usage as if they were alternating phases of reaction in a single personality. The preoccupations with thinking in the compulsive individual are not actually obsessive however. The essence of obsessiveness lies in the automaticity of meanings, and this direct flow between feeling and meaning remains open because the individual is fascinated with his own sensual self-awareness. The compulsive individual becomes lost in thought because he uses the manipulative component of thinking to avoid a self-awareness which tends to sexualize itself. He is actually engaged in analytic thinking, but he cannot reach an expanding world of experience in the process and thus is in the position of using imposing techniques for petty tasks.

The obsessive individual commits himself to patterns of action without a sense of exercising his will in the process, and the resultant activity does not have a true compulsive structure. The essence of the compulsive process lies in the fact that action is its own goal without the need to reach effective mastery, operating always within a restricted area which does not include an expanding interaction with others. The compulsive mechanism provides unobstructed access to a fragmented self-confidence. The obsessive individual is taken over by circumstances because he accepts an unselective commitment to patterns of action out of automatic feeling. He avoids a self-confidence which would be disturbing to his equilibrium because of its celebrative implications. He engages in manipulative activity which has an expanding and inventive structure, but he cannot reach expanding opportunity in the process. He finds himself bringing important conceptual images to emotionally impoverished interpersonal attachments.

Analytic thinking rests on faith in the emergence of truth. The task of analytic thinking ends when the truth stands revealed. Compulsive thinking finds no such endpoints because there is no truth with the necessary totality to produce a total submission in the thinker. Without the work which goes forward under the influence of faith, insights remain fragmented details which can never succeed in standing in the place of unity. Inventive manipulation rests on hope in the emergence of what is inevitable and right. The individual is set free from the devotion which energizes inventive manipulation when the right emerges. Obsessive involvements find no such endpoints because there is no right way which has the necessary permanence to release the man of action from his search. Without the enduring search for meaning which hope makes possible, mastery remains episodic and cannot find the continuity which confers importance on its accomplishments.

The only way that thinking can sustain the psychic investment which man's intellectual appetite brings to it is through the dedication of the entire personality to the task. The way a man lives determines the mechanisms of his thinking process. Analytic thinking can only find a creative channel when the individual rises to the challenge inherent in the service of an ideal. Submission to the ideal, with an accompanying capacity for faith in the ultimate unity and integrity of the idealized entity, can only be brought into being by love. Without love, thinking becomes self-serving and the integrity of the subject matter is destroyed. When men devote their great intellectual resources to the subject matter of human relationships, they enter an area of thought which makes great demands on their love capacities. If they rise to the occasion, this deepening of the self may initiate major growth processes within the personality, altering many facets of psychosocial adjustment, and thus disturbing established patterns of mature adaptation. If men turn away from the

challenge out of a sense of responsibility for maintaining
the adaptive accomplishments which they have already won,
the effort to think analytically in the great unknown areas
of the civilized personality deteriorates into compulsive
thinking. Under these conditions men lose their respect for
analytic thinking itself as applied to interpersonal relationships, and the resultant lack of a consistent and communicable body of insight is taken to be an inevitable state of affairs.
Each man becomes free to weave his own compulsive net of
pseudo-insights around his individual life, and the only ones
who succeed in representing themselves to be carriers of
human truths are usurpers who employ aggressive mechanisms.

The only way that manipulative activities can reach the
level of ability which man's constructive strivings require
is through the involvement of the whole personality in the
undertaking. The way a man lives becomes the basis of his
mode of operation in dealing with opportunity. Inventive
manipulation in the area of interpersonal control can only
find a creative outlet when the individual rises to the challenge inherent in unqualified involvement in large scale
opportunities. A dominant attitude toward reality with an
accompanying capacity for hopefulness in the ultimate value
of opportunity can only be brought into being by personal
power. Without inner power resources, manipulative activity
is taken over by egotistical vanity, and the assets and possessions which mastery has brought into being become transient
and evanescent. When men devote their constructive capacities to human interpersonal control, they enter an area of
psychological involvement which makes great demands on
their ability to sustain personal power. If they rise to the
occasion, this invigoration of the inner self tends to initiate
growth processes and brings alterations in the established
patterns of adaptive maturity. If men turn away from the
challenge out of their need for social stability, the experi-

mental approach in dealing with the chaotic areas of civilized interaction fails to attain genuine inventiveness and is invaded by obsessive preoccupations. Under these conditions men no longer attempt to bring the immorality of their social world under control, and the resultant loss of integrity in the elaboration of mastery is taken to be an inevitable consequence of civilized life. Each man becomes free to accept the obsessive encirclement which his own pseudo-mastery creates, and the only ones who emerge as examples to others of the right in human affairs are those who become expert at rationalizing and justifying their passive denial of the existence of wider horizons.

CREATIVE THINKING AND ACTING

When men expose themselves to the unknown and the chaotic in the world, they run the risk of a loss of their inner equilibrium. If the fear engendered by the unknown and the rage provoked by the chaotic are not to make inroads in the personality, there must be a way to grow within the self in relationship to the challenge of the undertaking, expanding the assets brought by the self to the point where they are equal to the task. Only in the presence of growth does the personality accept the kind of involvement with the unknown and the chaotic which excludes adaptive needs and purposes. In this way they lose their alien quality and become areas where man's honesty and courage can bring new knowledge and ability into existence.

It is impossible to think creatively without surrendering adaptive involvement with the subject of thought, and this means a purely contemplative relationship in which access to inventive manipulation disappears from the personality in that context. The depth of feeling which is brought by love is essential to this surrender. Only love has the necessary psychological qualities required to banish the need for power from the field. With power strivings gone, analytic thinking becomes free to engage the unknown.

It is impossible to act creatively without putting aside adaptive involvement with the materials and resources which are being manipulated, and this means that access to analytic thinking disappears from the personality in that context. The vigor of attitude which is conferred by power is essential to this spontaneous separation from the burdens of conceptual thought. Only power has the necessary psychological qualities to eliminate the otherwise pervasive influence of love. With love neutralized, the inventive manipulative talents are set free to engage the chaotic.

The kind of imbalance which creativity requires must attain a stable equilibrium within its own area of operation, and this means its goals must be separate from the adaptive life of the individual. Truth can only be its own end when there is sufficient capacity for privacy to permit the work of truth seeking to proceed. This state of selective withdrawal comes and goes according to the circumstances of life and never takes over the part of the self which is committed to the adaptive needs. The right can only be its own end when there is sufficient dissociation in relationship to worldly commitments to permit the dedication of the self to its creative undertakings. This state of mobile indifference is not allowed to encroach on the basic loyalties which maintain the social conformity of the individual.

Creative goals increase self-awareness and self-confidence and are the ultimate source of contentment and happiness in the life of the civilized individual. There is always room for more understanding and more capacity to take responsibility when truth and right are ends in themselves. If men become self-aware only through the kind of love that has adaptive value, they must become manipulative in the search for love and end in a competitive struggle for its rewards. If men become self-confident only through the kind of personal power that expresses itself in adaptive ways, the reaching for power is confined to areas where the responses of others can be taken for granted, becoming converted into exhibitionistic vanity and a hunger for popularity.

The permanence of truth eliminates its competitive qualities. The truth speaks for itself and although the individual is the vehicle of bringing it into existence, his words are inherently communicable without regard to the social identity he has attained. The integrity of the right gives it an existence which is independent of the personal self-expression which is its vehicle. The modes of action of the individual who embodies the right are inherently demonstrable and subject to imitative identification without regard to his social identity.

Love is only a meaningful force in interpersonal relationships when it leads to an increase in understanding which then becomes the permanent property of all men, and the instrument of this expansion of the influence of love is analytic thinking. The special problem in the pursuit of human understanding is sexuality since love for people in general brings the individual into the area of potential sexualization in a way that does not occur in the love of impersonal entities.

Power is only a force of value in interpersonal relationships when it leads to an increased capacity for responsibility which then becomes an irreducible part of the morality of all men, and the instrument of this expansion of the scope of power is inventive manipulation. The special problem in the development of human responsibility is the celebrative tendencies, since a power posture in relationship to society as a whole invites celebrative phenomena in a way that does not occur in the mastery of impersonal entities.

PART II

CREATIVE MATURITY

CREATIVITY AND SOCIAL PROGRESS

If the individual is to have a creative identity in relationship to society, his surplus feelings and attitudes cannot be captured by the mature social roles which are the carriers of his adaptive social adjustment. If he is to love the world of human beings around him, this love must emerge as a deep feeling which he finds out of the growing part of himself, and it must be directed toward individuals with whom he interacts and not toward an impersonal concept of society in general. Only then can love be a bridge to meaningful social experience and keep access to growth open for the individual himself. If he is to assume a power attitude toward others, his personal power must emerge as an impelling attitude which is the product of his personal growth, and it must attach itself to particular individuals and not be dissipated by an undifferentiated reaction to society as a whole. Only then can power reach genuine social involvements and keep access to growth open in the life of the individual.

Love becomes important to the individual and to those he loves when its full idealizing potential is fulfilled. Under these conditions love becomes the vehicle of the search for truth and leads not only to the inner development of the individual but becomes an expanding influence in the lives of others. Love which accepts no arbitrary limits is a permanent force in the lives of all those who are involved by it.

It is the work of love which makes it important and this consists of bringing new insights into being. Although insights are evolved from experience with particular individuals, they have a universal and communicable identity in the affairs of men. The substance of love is conceptual and in this form belongs to all men.

Power becomes important to the individual and those who belong to him when its full potential for providing a basis for experience is fulfilled. When power is ready to accept commitments, it becomes the instrument of reaching for the right and leads not only to the inner development of the individual but becomes an expanding influence in the lives of others. Power which accepts no arbitrary limits finds unity and integrity in the lives of those who are involved by it. It is the loyalties which personal power brings into being that make it important. The commitments of power create resources for mutual exploitation among men, bringing new mastery into being, and although this mastery is evolved from particular human situations, it has completeness in itself which is objectively demonstrable in any appropriate set of circumstances. The substance of power lies in its inevitability and in this form it is accessible to all men.

Love and power must retain their conceptual and methodological essence while keeping access to growth through full scale interpersonal involvements. Love must be free to withdraw from that which is unlovable if its work is to proceed, but this withdrawal is selective and in the service of privacy, remaining the choice of the individual. If the withdrawal becomes an established part of the psychological life of the individual, love cannot become aware of the totality of experience. Power must retain the right to become indifferent to forces which cannot be controlled if its capacity for loyalty is to be protected, but this indifference rests on the mobile capacity to dissociate the self from intransigent situations and remains an elective attitude. If indifference invades the personality, power cannot find the permanent aspects of human interactions.

Insight and mastery are the products of the psychological growth of individuals who are interacting with other individuals under the influence of love and power. Insight attains generality of a permanent nature; mastery finds effectiveness which is complete. The accumulation of insights which diminish the unknown in human affairs and the overcoming of the chaotic in human interactions through the establishment of mastery constitute the tools by which men build social progress. Insight and mastery are assets which come to mankind as a gift from the growth struggles of particular individuals. Social progress is an adaptive application of the accomplishments which individual creativity has brought into being, and the practical development of social understanding and control is never an end in itself.

MATURITY AND THE SURPLUSES

The idealization which underlies both love and creative thought is always vulnerable to sexualization. Depth of feeling sexualizes when it becomes aware of a feeling surplus in an individual who embodies the ideal. The constructive exploitation of resources underlies both personal power and creative action, and it is always vulnerable to a celebrative overflow. Vigor of attitude becomes celebrative when the need to be possessed is manifested in a surplus form by an individual who is the embodiment of unlimited responsiveness, under conditions of mutual involvement.

The work of love is not sexual. On the other hand, if the creative orientation of the self is bought at the price of desexualizing the self, the awareness of the sexual nature of man is damaged, and the ultimate unity of the human ideal cannot be comprehended. Idealization is not possible unless the entire range of phenomena contained within the ideal is accessible to the submissive awareness of the thinker.

The commitments of power are not celebrative, but if the creative organization of the self pays the price of renunciation of celebrative experience, the sharing of self-confident interaction with others is damaged and the sense of the enduring nature of human responsiveness is lost. The access to unlimited exploitation of opportunity must supply the individual with his sense of reality. Under these conditions all aspects of responsiveness in the environment are within the reach of the dominant self-confidence of the man of action, and he does not exclude the celebrative nature of human beings.

Sexuality is a pure state of automatically communicable feeling which guarantees unobstructed empathy and cohesion. Sexuality disappears when psychological work must be done and reappears when insight sets the individual free of his psychological task. No matter how much the individual may be involved in problem-solving mental activity, he can always return to a base of inner security where his previously attained insights confer a basic contentment. Within this area where there is respite from mental tension, he finds the repose which sexuality requires. The depth of feeling within himself which has been aroused by his creative interaction with the world provides a favorable ground for the emergence of sexuality. Access to a sexual life which does not encroach where it does not belong makes the whole process a harmonious one. If there is no room for sexuality, the personality guards against its emergence, and the depth of the character must ultimately be damaged.

Celebration is a pure mood of untrammeled access to elevated spirits which invokes automatic identification and cooperation. Celebration disappears when a sense of dutiful commitment must be accepted and reappears when mastery sets the individual free of his feeling of responsibility. No matter how much the individual may be involved in activities which explore the overcoming of obstacles, he can always lay his purposes temporarily aside and return to a base of inner freedom where his previously attained mastery confers a continuing happiness. Within this area where there is surcease from the holding of undischarged energies, he finds the spontaneity which gives access to celebration. The vigor of attitudes within himself which has been aroused by his creative interaction with the world provides a favorable ground for the emergence of celebration. When he can attain a fulfilling celebrative life which does not encroach where it does not belong, he can adjust himself to the phasic nature of harmonious celebration. If celebration becomes a threat to his capacity for devotion to mature goals, his personality becomes organized to exclude celebrative phenomena and the vigor of the character is ultimately compromised.

The tendency toward desexualization of the character is a pathological process and is the fundamental source of neurotic phenomena. The excess of feeling which cannot find a satisfactory attachment in neurotic processes results in an inner intensity which floats freely within the personality, leading to anxiety and a secondary sexualization which is compulsive in nature. The tensions which flow into a sexual channel are not actually sexual in origin. The neurotic develops tension in a creative pattern in areas where there are no genuine interpersonal problems and therefore no real need for creative intellectual work.

The tendency toward the exclusion of celebration from the character is a pathological process and is the fundamental source of delinquent phenomena. The excess of potential for action which cannot find expression in delinquent processes results in an inner vigor which has a dissociated existence within the personality, leading to restlessness and a secondary release of celebration. It finds obsessive outlets in an addicted pattern, attempting to channel energies which are not actually celebrative in origin. The delinquent develops energy accumulations in a creative pattern where there is no challenge from genuine obstacles in interpersonal relationships and cannot make a lasting creative commitment to any undertaking.

ADOLESCENCE AND MATURITY

The character which is formed in the growing child by family life comes into a developmental crisis with the onset of puberty. The adolescent must learn to deal with biological surpluses which are an inherent threat to creative interactions with others while establishing an inner identity in relationship to the world. This process must be carried out in an atmosphere of ignorance and neglect. Society as a whole takes an affirmative position on the place of the surpluses only in conventional mature heterosexual relationships. Adaptation in this area is suported but it is seen as an established entity without the encouraging of awareness or control of the developmental steps which are required to reach it. If the individual is to reach his adaptive heterosexuality in one great stride he must sacrifice much of his own psychological growth in the process. If he lingers along the way, expecting his surplus life to find its own destiny out of genuine feelings and experiences, he may find that conventional patterns of adaptation in this area have lost their inevitability or even their attractiveness.

Character specialization into yielding and assertive types provides the psychological means for reaching a maximum of individual autonomy without loss of capacity for a full participating interaction with other human beings. The autonomy of the specialized character rests on imbalance in the self and imposes a need to reach for balance through the utilization of dependent mechanisms. The development of the sexual and celebrative life in adolescence must avoid excesses of dependence, which tend to efface the inner identity, and extremes of autonomy, which threaten the individual's adaptive capacities. A highly developed character always tends to place the individual outside the mundane considerations of daily adaptive living. He is fully prepared to deal with the larger problems and obstacles of social living but tends to minimize his contact with the immediate environment.

The highly developed sensitivity of a yielding personality readily flows into sexuality but a spontaneous celebrative capacity is not readily reached and a great deal of dependence is required for the search. The highly developed spontaneity of an assertive personality gives immediate access to celebration, but a sufficiently deep sexual capacity has to be found in an experimental setting with much dependent help. There are several pathways which sex and celebration can take in the evolving maturity of adolescence. If the crisis arising from the emergence of the surpluses is temporarily pushed aside through the mechanism of desexualization and celebrative renunciation in the individual's relationships with others, a basis is laid for an excessive secrecy in sexual matters and a marked dissociation in the celebrative life, leading to neurosis and delinquency. In these pathological conditions, the surpluses exist in a free-floating form, preserving for the moment the existence of the childhood love and power patterns, but placing a great burden on the future development of creative interpersonal relationships. The free-floating surpluses are highly vulnerable to shame and guilt in a form which cannot find resolution through insight and mastery.

Another pathway is utilized by individuals who reach a socially supported surplus life directly without inner elaboration. To do this they must accept a relationship with the world which asks no fundamental personal questions and puts aside any significant challenging of the conventional social identity. Nothing is allowed to interfere with the finding of balance within the self. The surface characteristics of yielding personalities become very masculine, whereas the readily visible aspect of assertive personalities takes on a socially submissive and dutiful coloration. This all-encompassing drive to be mature may make a false passage into the pseudo-maturity of aggression and passivity, and under such conditions society as a whole pays the price of the individual's success in growing up. In perfectly balanced individuals, sexuality does not tend to attach itself to the desexualized love capacities and is therefore no great problem to the social interactions of the individual. All sexuality follow a familial pattern, and each one loves someone psychologically like himself. Such love has little work to do and thrives only in the encouraging atmosphere of romantic feelings. Love and hate are never very far apart. Celebration in the perfectly balanced personality does not tend to attach itself to the non-celebrative power capacities and therefore does not impose a serious burden on social control. Celebrative experience follows a familial pattern of mutual identification among those whose similarity makes such cooperation automatic. Such power drives do not search for new and creative commitments, but thrive on an adventuresome atmosphere of contrived challenges, being dissipated in activities in which the individual competes with others or against impersonal hazards in a spirit of play. Power and anger are never very far apart.

Another major pathway of development of sex and celebration in adolescence is to be found in the creative relationship with the world, and in this interaction the personality uses essentially mated mechanisms. If sex is to have a subsidiary relationship to love and be contained by it, then the growing personality must be free to develop the love capacities without arbitrary limits. Individual psychological growth through love utilizes all the idealizing resources of the self. The ideal must be a worthy one and can never be a mere reflection of the self if interaction with the world is to be preserved. Creative love responds to embodiments of power and carries the individual outside the limits of familial relationships.

If celebration is to be a subsidiary aspect of personal power, the growing personality can only contain its manifestations when it is free to develop the power capacities without pre-established limits. Individual psychological growth through personal power uses all the resources for involvement in opportunity which the personality can command. The exposure of the self to the exploitable value of opportunities must be genuine and can never be a mere echo of the established involvements if interaction with the world is to maintain its creative meaning. Creative power is attracted to the responsive situations which love brings into being and carries the individual into human interactions which lie outside family ties.

ADOLESCENT GROWTH AND THE MATED MECHANISMS

The depth of feeling in sexuality can be the natural consequence of depth of feeling in love. Sexuality cannot in itself build depth of character and if sexuality is used as an empathetic bridge to another person where deep ties are otherwise lacking, it can be destructive of the development of the love capacities. Romantic love is based on empathetic feelings between individuals who see themselves reflected in each other. Such love thrives on withdrawal from the world of problems where faith and analytic thinking are required. The pleasures of romance justify its selfishness and often lead lovers to feel that the outer world is a hostile place.

Behind romantic intensity lies a shallowness in the creative love capacities.

The vigor of attitude in celebrative experience can be the natural overflow of the vigor developed by personal power. Celebration cannot in itself build vigor in the character, and if it is used to attract the identification of others where mutual commitments do not create the gregarious spirit, it can be destructive of the development of the power capacities. Adventuresome power is based on undertakings which arouse the mutual admiration of the participants. Such power thrives on indifference toward the world of obstacles where hope and enduring inventiveness in human affairs are required, and it needs an aura of the inherently glorious. The enjoyment inherent in adventure justifies its vanity and often leads to an emphasis on the unworthiness of the mundane world because it constitutes a threat to its elevated spirits. Behind adventuresome spontaneity lies a weakness in the creative power capacities.

When the adolescent personality seeks to find its own relationship to the world, it must employ mechanisms of self-development in which sexuality does not interfere with the growth of the love capacities and celebration does not substitute itself for the search for an expanding personal power. When love and power develop through a relationship with mankind in general, the integrity and continuity of the growth process are assured. When love reaches outside the family circle and its extensions in the community to expose itself to the impact of a living world which is not concerned with the security of any particular individual, the idealizing process not only has work to do but becomes an essential part of maintaining interpersonal relationships. Unprotected exposure to the impact of experience does not mean that the individual is without selectivity, but he does not cease to maintain the faith which permits him to accept the totality of experience. He hates what he cannot love and withdraws only to protect his love capacities.

When power extends itself beyond the limits of family attachments to find novel opportunity in the outside world, it leaves the established patterns of freedom behind. The need to exploit resources not only becomes the motivation for exploring the nature of the world but becomes an essential element in maintaining interpersonal relationships. The unqualified willingness to risk the inner identity in commitment to new loyalties does not mean that the individual gives up his access to mobility, but no matter how much he must live in terms of the realities of the moment, he does not cease to maintain hope in the permanent nature of worldly involvements. He responds with anger to that which he cannot make his own and accepts indifference only to protect his power capacities.

If the individual is to grow, he must live in a changing world. The insights and mastery of creative individuals bring new truth and right into being, and although they set in motion the forces of change which ultimately bring social progress, the creative individual does not depend upon such social alterations. The changing world which the creative individual needs comes to him out of his own personal growth. There is no such thing as personal growth without expansion of the scope of the interpersonal world in which the individual lives. Love is a hungry emotional state which is always ready to include more human experiential phenomena within its awareness. Power is an eager attitude which is always receptive to a further exploitation of human resources. The sexualization of love through romantic attachments provides for the gratification of an appetite which has no relationship to an expanding world. The celebrative utilization of power through adventuresome undertakings provides for accomplishments which have no relationship to expanding interpersonal involvements.

MATURITY AND DEPRESSION

The self gains its inner identity from the surplus in warmth or pride with which the individual faces the world. This surplus is kept alive by interpersonal interactions which can only have the necessary continuity and integrity if the individual is prepared to find beauty and goodness in the world out of his own psychological resources. Any individual can feel warmth if others love him, but such a state of empathetic feelingfulness can only have an assured continuity in dependent psychological states. Dependence on the love of others for maintenance of the inner identity leads to interpersonal crises in which the individual seeks to control the feeling of others for the preservation of his mental health. He demands love so that he may remain a loving person. This is a childlike position which can only increase his dependence. It undermines the meaning of love and ends both the capacity for inner growth and the expanding awareness of beauty in the world.

The surplus in pride of the assertive individual can maintain itself if others are devoted to its enforcement, but such a power attitude can only remain uncompromising in dependent psychological states. Dependence on the admiration of others for the maintenance of the inner identity leads to interpersonal crises in which seductive means of winning identification are used to protect the individual from an emergence of antisocial impulses. His ability to attract responsive feeling becomes a tool in the preservation of his power status. This kind of appeal for help rests on the arousal of pity and is a childlike technique which undermines the value of personal power. It is an unfavorable atmosphere for inner growth and does not lead into an expanding exploitation of the goodness of the world.

The surpluses which underlie character identity can only find the self-fulfillment which brings contentment and hap-

piness when they lead to inner growth in a changing interpersonal world. In order to maintain creative interpersonal
relationships, the individual must be able to deal with the
tendency for the love surplus to sexualize and the power
surplus to be invaded by celebration. He must also be able
to deal with the impact of depression on the adaptive relationships of his mature social life.

The transition from adolescent curiosity and eagerness into
mature wisdom and strength must be made without failure
in adaptive effectiveness and without loss of creative flexibility in interpersonal relationships. This means that adaptive maturity must remain limited in its psychic investment,
utilizing only as much of the self as is required to attain
the desired goals. This process of reserving part of the self
cannot proceed at the cost of ignoring and bypassing any
part of the adaptive requirements. Qualitatively speaking,
the individual must meet all adaptive challenges with the
necessary tension and energy, but in quantitative terms he
never invests more than is necessary for the practical purposes at hand. In a complex society his adaptive undertakings may be of great variety and may at times consume all
of his psychological capacities, but this state of affairs is not
allowed to stabilize itself into a fixed pattern of living. If
creative selectivity and mobility must be pushed aside in
favor of the practical necessities of mature stability, it is as
if the individual is committed to dealing with an emergency
situation without being able to make a place for the fear
and rage reactions which belong to emergencies. Social maturity is a basic essential of living which he cannot choose
to abandon in the face of difficulties. If the emergency never
ends and he is forced by life circumstances to accept its
consequences as if they were an inevitable aspect of his life,
he is vulnerable to a loss of inner identity. If the individual
must give up inner intensity and vigor with its accompanying contentment and happiness as part of the requirements

of maturity, he must fall victim to depression. The acceptance of an autocratic and dogmatic maturity from which
there is no escape or appeal destroys the autonomy of the
individual.

The acceptance of a tyrannical maturity ends the possi-
bility of living in a changing interpersonal world. Security
is eternally wedded to doing what is supposed to be right
and the modalities of the right cannot change. Freedom
comes out of the sense of belonging which the acceptance of
unquestioned truth confers and the structure of the apparent
truth cannot change. The individual becomes a cog in a
social machine who must try to raise his flattened emotional
level by empathetic reinforcement of his self-love with others
who feel similar inadequacies, or he must struggle to elevate
his mood by cultivating mutual admiration among those who
share his social entrapment. Socially supported self-love and
vanity take advantage of perverse and addicted mechanisms
which are not identified for what they are since they enter
the accepted image of the self as molded by the social role.

DEPRESSION AND MENTAL HEALTH

Adolescence is a period of self-exploration and discovery.
Maturity is reached when the self conforms to those patterns
of interaction with others which the various social roles
require. The independent and highly individual self is
used in this adaptation, and if its identity is to survive it
cannot make sacrifices which are not essential to the adaptive requirements. In a changing external world the requirements of maturity do not remain fixed and unalterable, but
they do not change in response to the individual's need to
express his individuality. If mental health and social conformity are to evolve together in the psychological growth
of the individual, they must be won by a gradual learning
process in which the self gains maximum expression without

doing violence to basic social standards. The difficulties in becoming mature cannot be overcome by embracing maturity without restraint or reservation. Maturity is contaminated by all the perversity, addiction, falseness, and immorality which men have been forced to accept in order to find personal rewards in their social roles. This is the price men have paid for their civilized accomplishments. Unless the door remains open to change in the structure of maturity, creative investment of the self in interpersonal relationships becomes meaningless. Truth and right in human affairs must ultimately find access to social ideas and institutions, bringing changes when the pressure brought by the growth of individuals has prepared the community for it. Truth and right have an inherent importance which gives them an impelling influence in the community even when relatively few individuals are the embodiment of their existence, whereas outmoded ideas and institutions have a diminishing capacity for attracting anything more than lip service and outward conformity. There are always transitional phases in a progressive society which lead men to believe that the new generation is lacking in the capacity to adhere to the established standards of maturity, but it is not the acceptance of maturity which is at fault but rather the inability of the older generation to comprehend the nature of the individual search for maturity in a changing society.

A changing world threatens the mental health and social conformity of individuals who have given up their independent capacity for personal psychological growth. Since social change of a creative kind is not initiated by external social pressures but by the need of particular individuals to live in a better human world, and especially by their need to leave a better world behind them for the benefit of future generations, those individuals who find themselves fully committed to the social ideas and institutions into which they were born can only experience a diminishing involvement in the life of their time. This kind of reduced interpersonal invest-ment of the self leads to the flattened affect and retardation of mood which characterizes the two kinds of pathological depression.

Since emptiness of feeling reduces the self-awareness, the flattened affect type of depression is not readily recognized by intuitive means. The individual has a vague hunger for emotional commitment which remains unfocused until the secondary manifestations usher in the clinical illness. Mood depressions are more readily seen because the retardation is evident in interpersonal reactions, but again such states are readily mistaken for a healthy need for privacy until secondary symptoms reveal their essential pathology.

Emptiness of feeling leads to distortions in the self-aware-ness, so that fatigue and hypochondriacal awareness of frag-mented inner sensations come to the fore. Reduction in mood level distorts the self-confidence so that chronic bore-dom and a sense of helplessness takes possession of the per-sonality. Shame characterizes loss of feeling, and guilt ac-companies the inability to act. Once the secondary mani-festations of depression have established themselves, the symptoms of the two types mingle and differentiation be-comes difficult.

DEPRESSION AND THE SURPLUSES

The fusion of the creative and the adaptive capacities of the self is the psychological task of adolescence. The highly creative adolescent delays his maturity because his auton-omy provides him with the means to reach maturity in his own way and he needs the time and flexibility which delay provides. He does not attempt to distort the basic tenets of maturity but alters the manner and degree of his involve-ment with them. Chronically dependent individuals who

cannot adequately comprehend or manage mature requirements may appear to have similar personality traits, but their
clinging to familial supports brings neurotic and delinquent
manifestations, and the overcoming of this dependence often
precipitates them into a tyrannically mature world. Neurosis
and delinquency delay maturity but not for the sake of inner
growth. There are areas of overlapping traits common to
both creative individuals and chronically dependent persons,
arising from their non-conformist and skeptical tendencies
in adolescence. It is only when the goals of inner growth
make themselves manifested in the life of the creative individual that the difference becomes clear. Any breakdown
in the creative process whether temporary or permanent
can bring neurotic and delinquent manifestations just as
any overinvolvement in the patterns of maturity at any time
of life can bring depressive manifestations.

Adolescent sexuality and celebration remain unattached
and continue to develop in a pattern which is essentially
mated in nature. The internal psychological growth of adolescence reaches toward love and power as goals in themselves. The intensity of idealization which pure love brings
to the personality readily overflows into private sexual feeling and is utilized in autoerotic phenomena. It is typical of
creative love that it brings unattached sexuality into being
with associated autoerotism. This kind of acceptance of
sexuality as a thing in itself is essential to the further growth
of the love capacities. The spontaneity which power uses
for the exploitation of reality readily overflows into a dissociated celebrative mood. It becomes self-releasing, detach-
ing the individual from the immediate influence of conventional discipline and loyalties. In such psychological states
the individual seeks playful enjoyment for its own sake,
using his personal appetites and momentary needs as a complete guide to interests and activities.

As men come into maturity they seek to engage their

sexual and celebrative life in the unmated patterns of family life. The sexuality which was born in idealization now seeks an object which is not to be idealized, and the celebration which owes its origin to the sense of free access to opportunity must now accept a partnership without exploitation. As long as there is no psychological overinvestment in the marriage, the two partners can bring a sexual and celebrative capacity to each other which has a prior origin and which continues to be fed by interpersonal interactions in the world. If idealization and exploitation invade the marriage to an extent where the mature adaptive function of the marital relationship is undermined, the participants are not only cut off from the world but they expose themselves to serious disappointment which undermines their creative capacities. Under such conditions, the marriage cannot perform the social functions required of it.

The unmated attachments to persons psychologically like the self form the bulwark of family structure. All the mature functions of the family are served by such relationships, but the surpluses which are required to deepen and enliven the personality are exposed to a struggle for existence. Sex and celebration take their place in family life through a system of prohibitions and permissive channels of encouragement. The prohibitions are rigid and arbitrary, such as the prohibition against incest, and the permissiveness does not stop with releasing inherent tendencies but undertakes to stimulate and guide, following fixed patterns which are taken for granted. Because every mature individual lives in the shadow of a potential depression which he must personally resist, society provides a background of customs and conventions designed to stimulate acceptable sexual responsiveness and celebrative release. The test of the appropriateness of these feelings and attitudes lies in their harmonious relationship to the social patterns of maturity, and any source of sexual pleasure and celebrative enjoyment which does not lead men away from their stable social commitments is automatically acceptable. The community is self-preserving and seeks to maintain a maximum of stability with a minimum of rebellion and heresy. Society has no direct stake in social progress. Without the pressure toward change coming from creative individuals, society would continue to cover up difficulties and employ superficial patchwork remedies for the disorders of civilized psychological life. Especially where the sexual and celebrative surpluses are involved, society finds it easy to ignore and bypass truth and right, since it is primarily concerned with maintaining a level of access to pleasure and enjoyment which will keep depression at bay and preserve the psychological stability of its members.

THE WAR BETWEEN MEN AND WOMEN

The social roles of masculinity and femininity in the civilized world utilize biological masculinity and femininity only insofar as the interests of the family union are served thereby. The general tendency in the western world is for men to be the embodiment of social maturity while seeking as much secret and dissociated expression of the surpluses as possible, and for women to attract and involve men through the calculated utilization of surplus tendencies while directing their real efforts toward maintaining the stable and mature structure of society. This state of affairs tends to create a social differentiation between men and women into which masculine and feminine traits are projected, but which has no necessary relationship to the biological differences between them. In spite of the surface maturity of men and the apparently indulged role of women, men tend to become the carriers of the creative processes and women the sponsors of stable family feelings and attitudes, and this leads to the social depreciation of women in worldly contexts and to the formation of an image of masculinity which includes much psychological content which is secret and separate. The psychological interaction between male creativity and female stability makes men and women more valuable to each other in establishing a mature adjustment and in overcoming depressive manifestations, but it also lays the basis for psychological warfare between the sexes. The price of creativity in a man may be the reduction or elimination of women's influence in his life, just as the price of maturity in a woman may be the refusal to respect the extra-familial preoccupations of men, in which case men are seen as immature beings whose impractical dreams and postures can only be tolerated as an unfortunate aspect of family necessity.

The unknown and the chaotic in human affairs cannot be faced on a crisis basis. The individual cannot pick up such preoccupations as a practical means of promoting the goals of maturity when threats to adaptive success exist, and then lay them aside when the pressure of the crisis subsides. Creativity is a lifetime matter, and the degree of commitment is determined by the inner acceptance of the challenge of the general human problems and obstacles to be overcome. When truth and right emerge, they do so in their own time and place without regard to the practical needs of a mature social adjustment. Insofar as women are the keepers of the mature social goals through their preoccupation with family welfare, they tolerate the creativity of men as a potential source of wisdom and strength in family life. Although the family can utilize the creative resources of its members in some contexts, it cannot be the source of these capacities. The greater the scope of the creative life, the more conflict results from the attempt to measure it to the dimensions of practical family goals. Insofar as men undertake to maintain a clear inner identity in the search for truth and right, they tend to make a retreat or accept an enlistment. In so doing, the acceptance of the basic standards of maturity tends to weaken where family life is concerned, and family attachments, if they exist at all, are utilized as an expendable asset in a socially unstable life.

Maturity thrives when balance becomes the exclusive goal of human development. Yielding personalities diminish neurotic symptoms through total involvement with socially supported action, putting aside the tendencies toward withdrawal through emphasis on the masculine aspects of their social role. The feminine role of the woman in family life supports the male involvement in action, but this role can only be effective when it is used for the immediate practical purposes of the family itself. Any tendency for such masculinity to reach toward a creative relationship with the world becomes a threat both to family stability and to the mental health of the marital partners. A masculine role which is reached by arrangement and agreement has no genuine autonomy and cannot tolerate the kind of frustrations in the external world which can only be successfully met through the use of an enduring courage and hopefulness. Artificial and contrived masculinity maintains its genuine appearance only in the context which brings it into being. Outside this magical circle it is vulnerable to a loss of self-control, rage, hypomanic compensatory strivings, and immorality.

When the assertive personality makes balance the exclusive goal of psychological development, it overcomes delinquent patterns of behavior through the use of socially supported feeling, putting aside the tendency toward indifference through permanent commitment to the feminine aspects of the social role. The woman in family life becomes the law-giver who accepts responsibility for the reinforcement of social ideas, beliefs, and principles. These concepts have nothing to do with truth seeking but gain their permanence through usefulness in maintaining family stability. In the process of reinforcing and defending familial cohesion, the woman takes on a manipulative function within the family circle which has its sources in a basically masculine identity. If the man attempts to use the feminine aspect of himself in a creative relationship with the external world, the shallowness of feeling leads to a sentimentalization which threatens both family stability and the capacity of the partners for social conformity. A feminine orientation which exists only because of dependent social reinforcement under family influence can never find the autonomy required for meeting the kind of problems in the external world which require the application of wisdom and faith. Superficial and empathetic femininity can only influence the personality within the context which brings it into being. Outside the stable family structure which has been built by automatic loyalties, operating in a spirit of miraculous effectiveness, the feminine tendencies are vulnerable to loss of self-awareness, fear, schizoid detachment, and surrender to ignorance.

The war between the sexes waxes and wanes as the pendulum swings between tyrannical maturity and the kind of immaturity which threatens to bring neurosis and delinquency in its wake. Because women draw men into the commitments of maturity, they are expected by men to maintain a high level of pleasure and enjoyment in family life, sufficient to keep depression at bay. Because men involve women in their search for an autonomous inner identity, they are expected by women to bring so much wisdom and strength to the partnership that mental illness and antisocial tendencies cannot emerge. When these tasks prove impossible of accomplishment within the scope of family relationships, mutual hatred and anger become a permanent feature of the marital relationship.

THE WAR BETWEEN ADOLESCENTS
AND ADULTS

The creative productivity of individuals has a gradually spreading influence which first alters the thinking and acting of others only in the area of their private feelings and separate attitudes. Basic social ideas and institutions do not change until there is a sufficient accumulation of new truth and right so that the transition can be made from the old to the new without loss of continuity in the basic requirements of maturity.

During adolescence the search for an inner identity exposes the individual to the creative influences at work in the adult society around him. Social progress is facilitated by the pressure brought by the dissatisfactions of the adolescent with the status quo. The adult world may respond to this pressure as if it were the product of rebellion and heresy even though it may be a simple adherence to a higher level of social understanding and responsibility. The resulting conflict between adolescents and adults leads to the formation of an adolescent community with its own beliefs and modes of behavior. The existence of an adolescent society with its own internally reinforced social identity creates a hiatus which tends to reduce the influence of adolescents on society in general and is therefore acceptable to those who oppose social change. When adolescents must make their own world in a specialized society of their own, much of their creative potential is compromised. The adolescent needs the kind of teaching and leadership which makes a place for his independent creative search. When his dependent requirements are met through the operation of an adolescent society, the primary emphasis comes on dissatisfaction with the adult world rather than on the continuity and integrity of the search for truth and right. The greater the emphasis on an adolescent social identity, the more the surface characteristics of youthfulness are emphasized, provided these character-istics are shared in common by the group. This kind of pseudo-maturity is as tyrannical as any adult maturity which is being rejected and stands as a barrier to the real goal of adolescent development which is the introduction of the growing personality into a mature world with the maximum of autonomous inner identity.

In adolescence the real problems and obstacles of the human environment come into focus, and the need for mean-ingful insights and mastery of value becomes a living part of the daily interpersonal life. When these necessary instru-ments for dealing with an expanding interpersonal world are found to be inadequate, the adolescent is forced toward a creative position in his own life with the accompanying tendency toward withdrawal and indifference. If these ten-dencies fail to provide a constructive relationship with the world, they deteriorate into neurotic and delinquent phe-nomena which may only find resolution through the aban-donment of the creative undertaking. Individuals who give up their adolescent strivings as the price of maturity look back on adolescence as a period of stress in an atmosphere of shame and guilt which was tolerated as a part of biological and social development. This view of themselves provides them with a ready made means of dealing with adolescent phenomena in the next generation. Insofar as the war be-tween adolescents and adults succeeds in establishing two separate camps with contrasting social identities, the creative capacities of the adolescent are compromised, and the influ-ence of the adolescent on social progress in the mature world is diminished.

THE ADOLESCENT COMMUNITY

Adolescence is the time when the search for an inner identity produces the first developmental utilization of the

full submissive and dominant capacities of the self. Idealization takes over the personality, just as the exploitation of
opportunity becomes an impelling need. The self-image is
sought with a great hunger for heightened feeling. Any in-
terruption in it becomes a psychic threat marked by self-
conscious pain. Self-control becomes a compelling requirement which is sought through heightened involvements, and
any diminution of self-control becomes a psychic threat characterized by anguish.

As the adolescent opens his heart to his own yielding tendencies he requires great understanding in order to attain
an expanding interface in his interaction with the world. If
his need for understanding keeps him in a childlike dependence, his growing self-awareness can only be disturbed.
What he really requires are genuine insights based on
knowledge of the human personality. Such understanding he
can use autonomously for his own purposes. His disappointment with the adult world at this point rests on the fact that
the wisdom he believed was there in his childhood is revealed
as inadequate.

As the adolescent undertakes to give full scope to his assertive tendencies, he must find a high level of personal responsibility if these tendencies are to find an expanding interface
in his interaction with others. The adolescent needs help in
establishing cooperation with others in a responsible fashion,
and he expects to be inducted into an expanding mastery
without being put in a dependent position in the process. If
he is patronized by helpful adults, his growing capacity for
self-control can only be compromised. What he really requires
are genuine techniques of mastery based on objectively demonstrable abilities in human affairs. Such modalities of
taking responsibility can be used by him in an autonomous
way for his own purposes. His frustration with adults in
this area comes from the fact that the moral strength he be-

lieved to exist when he was a child stands revealed in his adolescence to be inadequate to the task at hand.

Adults do not want adolescents to develop psychological needs which carry them outside the range of adult capacities for giving help and understanding, because this alienates the two groups and tends to unmask the ignorance and weakness which has been masquerading in the mature world as wisdom and strength. The adolescent challenge to the adult world can be very unsettling when mature stability is based on rigid adherence to arbitrary law and tyrannical authority. If the hiatus between the generations becomes great, the adolescent need for teaching and leadership results in a growing disorientation and disorganization in the adolescent personality. Withdrawal and indifference at this point are not based on faith and hope in alternatives, but on a disruption of communication and a loss of the basis for shared experience in those areas where the struggle for an identity is taking place. In order to maintain the high level of cohesive feeling and readiness for cooperation which adolescent development requires, an adolescent community comes into being in which the members provide teaching and leadership functions for each other. Since there is already a breakdown in the access to the kind of truth and right which exists externally to the self, the adolescent is put in the impossible position of applying his own insights and mastery at a time when they are struggling to come into existence. It is his fate to discover that there is no one so foolish as a wise man in a state of growth who utilizes the hypothetical in the place of established truth, and no one so unreliable as the strong man in search of the tools of self-fulfillment who uses experimental procedures in the place of established right. In these circumstances, the adolescent community can have neither continuity nor integrity, but tends to come in and out of focus and to fragment into sub-groups according to the needs of the moment. Adolescents have to protect them-

selves from too great an involvement with each other, and
for this purpose the educational system provides a setting
where flexible relationships can run their course. Through
attending school the adolescent maintains the goal of ultimate maturity while privileged to search on his own and
among his own kind for the kind of self-awareness and self-
confidence which can only come if he maintains privacy
and separation from the adult world.

The community of the young which is facilitated by the
educational system is helpful to adolescent development,
but it cannot overcome deficiencies which are beyond its
scope. If the individual becomes too involved with the
maturity aspects of education, namely in establishing a
superior competitive position in his vocational and social
development, he finds himself the prisoner of the arbitrary
and the tyrannical on a scale which exceeds that of the
world outside. Such a path leads to degrees of intimidation
and seduction which are highly destructive to the inner
identity, and are the breeding ground of malignant depressive phenomena. If the individual turns toward the
higher levels of interpersonal feeling and cooperation which
he needs, the tendency to be flooded by the psychological
surpluses becomes very great. Sex and celebration invade
love and power, and if he is not to turn away from his
growing capacities for human involvement, he must be
sure that the creative aspects of the warmth and vigor in
himself are not overwhelmed by their surplus expression.
The keeping of sex and celebration in place cannot be
done by making rules or supervising patterns of behavior.
Only the love that does psychic work can be bigger than
sexuality and thereby make a place for it, and only the
personal power which enriches mankind by increasing the
resources it exploits can contain celebration and therefore
be harmonious with it. Without the necessary access to

truth and right, sex and celebration must either overwhelm the creative development of love and power or be put under artificial controls which ultimately brings the search for an independent identity to an end.

ADOLESCENCE AND FAMILY LIFE

A conventional heterosexual adjustment requires the establishment of a domestic relationship in which the partners take over a variety of social roles arising from adaptive social requirements. In becoming a husband, a wife, a father, a mother, a wage earner, a homemaker, and a respected member of the community of those who take on similar roles, the individual makes a transition from the adolescent world of self-development into the mature world of stable social functions. If the adolescent is to bring his emerging inner identity to this adaptive task in such a way that his individuality is not effaced in the process, he must measure his commitments to the adaptive effort required. If the social roles take over the whole personality, the independent access to truth and right disappears, and human understanding and responsibility are channeled entirely by their usefulness in reinforcing family needs and goals.

Continuity and integrity within the context of family relationships are necessary assets of family life, and this kind of stability becomes the first concern of society as a whole. Society takes no direct responsibility for the creative development of any individual, and when the search for an inner identity comes into conflict with stable familial beliefs and modes of behavior, society cannot give active support to the individual, even if these beliefs are based on ignorance and the modes of behavior are immoral in their broad interpersonal implications. Familial cohesion has priority even if it employs perverse elements, and the loyalty to familial patterns of shared interests comes before individual self-expression even if familial gregariousness utilizes addicted mechanisms.

The heterosexual family relationship cannot absorb and utilize the full range of interpersonal psychological capacities which the individual brings to life. The developing love and power tendencies are oriented and organized for inter-action with each other in a mated pattern. The flowing of these powerful psychological forces into the mating of the lower animals accounts for the continuity and integrity of the domain. The arousal of these forces in adolescence ac-counts for the depth and vigor of the personality and brings continuity and integrity to the relationship of the individual and society. The impact of mated mechanisms in adolescence reaches an inner self which is not yet shielded by the balance inherent in the social roles. The great hunger of love for idealization, and the compelling drive of power for posses-sion of a responsive environment, take over the personality and involve the individual in an expanding world of self-consciousness and the exploratory testing of self-confidence. His finding of himself and his discovery of the world are one and the same psychological undertaking. It is only his own depth which can reveal the beauty outside himself, and only his own spontaneous vigor which can cause the goodness in the environment to materialize. Without such self-development he cannot live in an expanding world, and the adolescent process ceases to have genuine significance.

When adolescence is a highly productive period of inner growth, the transition into a conventional maturity may be tentative and incomplete since the independent individual must retain his selectivity and mobility if the transition is to be made without sacrifice of his psychological accom-plishments. At this point he must engage in a struggle with the familial patterns of empathy and the identifications which were established in his childhood. His psychological assets may also be used in the elaboration of mature social functions, and the more his development moves in a mature direction, the less alienation will occur between the individual and his family. No matter how much the family has contributed to the creative identity of the individual, it can never easily stand aside and permit the process of self-discovery to follow its own path. The loss of empathy and identification involved is perceived as a wound to family continuity and unity.

It is impossible to grow without privacy and separateness, and these psychic states require that the individual leave others behind. Sometimes hate and anger become the tools by which the separation is effected, but love is best equipped to make a selective withdrawal, and power alone can provide the necessary judgement for guiding the indifference which makes mobility possible. Love brings wisdom to the task, and power employs moral strength to find the way. The greater the divergence between the individual and his family which his growth brings into being, the less likely he is to take the patterns of maturity for granted. Some men spend a lifetime in what is essentially an adolescent state, refusing to make settlements which would endanger their inner identity. Most men make settlements which are rewarded in various ways, but difficulties emerge when they lose their awareness that a settlement has been made. It is helpful in maintaining mature social roles to believe in their inevitability and to adhere to them without qualification, but such feelings and attitudes cut off access to an expansion of truth and right in human affairs. When society itself changes in the course of social progress, men accept new ways of finding maturity, leaving yesterday's unquestioned beliefs and immutable modes of behavior behind in favor of an equal involvement in current standards and practices. The adolescent is exposed to a need for change which comes from forces within himself. As he alters his relationship to the world, the world he knows and experiences itself undergoes alteration. Out of this expansion he can find new truth and right which then becomes the substance of his creative contribution to society. Without such personal initiative coming from the inner psychic life of individuals, there can be no constructive social change.

ADOLESCENCE AND THE SURPLUSES

As the child enters puberty his biological capacity for deep sexual feeling and its accompanying orgastic discharge emerges, as does his capacity for the expression of vigorous and self-willed celebrative attitudes with their accompanying surrender to the circumstances of the moment. These biological channels of expression are engrafted upon the already existent depth of feeling and vigor of attitude which family life has brought to the developing personality of the child. One of these channels is primary in the character and the other has a secondary relationship to the self. Only one can confer an inner identity; the other is sought for the sake of balance. Biological maturation produces a great surge forward in the inner identity. The coming of mature sexuality increases not only the capacity to hold tension in a self-aware fashion, but also the range and complexity of interpersonal relationships. Sexuality brings depth to the fore, assuring the exposure of the sensitivity in the self to a widening interaction with the world. The coming of the mature celebrative capacities increases not only the ability to hold an accumulation of energy in a self-confident fashion, but also provides a readiness for exploitation of interpersonal opportunities. Celebration brings vigor to the fore, assuring the access of the spontaneity in the self to a continuity of involvement in the external world.

The sensitive yielding individual can accept the coming

of his orgastic sexual capacities more easily than he can his emerging potential for celebrative involvement since he is dependent in the area of his organization for action. In celebrative expression he is vulnerable to intimidation and guilt. The spontaneous assertive individual can accept the consequences of his emerging capacities for celebrative surrender more easily than he can the inner alterations which orgastic sexuality brings since he is dependent in the area of his orientation toward feeling attachments. In sexual expression he is vulnerable to seduction and shame.

As puberty ushers in psychological adolescence, a struggle is initiated on a broad scale to make a place for the surpluses as ends in themselves with a private and separate status in relationship to the adult world and divorced from the goals of the mature social roles. If the surpluses cannot be expressed in their own terms, the individual is forced to enter maturity with insufficient preliminary self-development. Assertive individuals tend to grow up too rapidly in their patterns of sexual expression. They are readily ensnared by fixed images of the masculine sexual role, being seduced into masculine commitments which allow no room for self-development on an autonomous basis. Yielding individuals tend to identify with conventional patterns of celebrative expression too readily, following the path established by socially supported permissiveness. They are intimidated by the prohibitions which lie outside the range of their approved activities, and their self-development suffers accordingly. Seduction can feminize an assertive personality at the very moment when the individual believes he is reaching the ultimate fulfillment of his masculine self-expression, and intimidation can lead a yielding personality into adopting a caricature of masculine spontaneity at the price of concealing all manifestations of inner sensitivity.

The search of the adolescent for sexual and celebrative

expression which comes naturally to him and which fulfills itself in its own terms cannot be limited to the prescribed patterns of family life. If the search for an inner identity enters the sphere of marriage, it can only undermine the stable structure which belongs to the function of the marital relationship. In his personal search for sex and celebration which is separate from its ultimate utilization in the mature social roles of marriage, the individual encounters a psychological area which is characteristically beset by ignorance and neglect in the civilized world. Men want to believe that marriage captures all the surplus tendencies of the partners in the same way that the mated relationship of the male and female does in nature. The feelings and attitudes which the social institution of marriage cultivates and protects for its own purposes have no necessary connection with what is true or right for the developing surplus life of the adolescent. The great romantic longings and adventuresome eagerness of the adolescent must be worked out on a sufficient scale in interpersonal relationships to include all their manifestations within the scope of self-awareness and self-control. There is an innate tendency for the beliefs and modes of behavior which are inherent in the institution of marriage to corrupt the developing capacities for personal honesty and courage. The more creative capacities the individual attains, the more resistive he is to the final and irrevocable commitments of the social roles, and if adaptive requirements break down this resistance, he may enter marriage as a personal and special undertaking in which he attempts to invest the full range of his creative capacities. If the marital partners seek a unique and individual accomplishment in their relationship, they undermine the nature of marriage itself and create a human situation where the greater psychic investment leads to a lesser chance of adaptive success.

THE NATURE OF THE UNATTACHED SURPLUSES

The unattached sex and celebration which are released in adolescence create a sense of alienation in the individual. If he is not to be victimized by fear and rage, he must find the insights and modalities of mastery which permit him to dissipate the unknown in himself and deal with the chaotic in his own nature. Society as a whole cannot nurture and protect what is essentially private and separate in his growing personality. What he needs and has a right to expect from society is that he will be provided with the conceptual tools and procedural techniques which alone can permit him to develop as an autonomous individual. What he actually gets from the adult world is a withholding of love when his emerging sexuality does not conform to the established patterns which the mature social role prescribes, and a rejection of continuity in group identifications when his emerging celebrative tendencies do not flow readily into the socially established channels. The withholding of love as a means of guiding the individual toward maturity results in a degradation of love itself, opening the doors to hate and ultimately to fear. Such interactions deprive the personality of the one essential element which can maintain the desexualization of love. Without the faith which love alone can bring, the unattached sexuality intrudes on human warmth whenever that warmth deepens, leaving the individual in the position of finding social adaptation through superficiality. The withholding of love as a means of control is intimidating in the extreme.

The refusal of participation in power expressions as a means of guiding the individual toward maturity results in a depreciation of power itself, exposing the personality to anger and ultimately to rage. Such rejections deprive the personality of the essential means of excluding celebrative overflow from power attachments. Without the hope that personal power alone can bring, the unattached celebrative energies intrude on human helpfulness whenever these co-operative activities are invested with an increase of vigor, and this puts the individual in a position where unconcern for others becomes the pathway to his social adaptation. The expulsion of the individual from group identification as a means of guiding his loyalties and attachments results in a helpless personality, and this mode of influencing others is seductive in the extreme.

There is a great longing for depth and an eager readiness for spontaneity in the psychological structure of adolescence. It is through enthusiasm and inspiration that the self becomes permanent and whole. Once these psychological states have been attained, they reach the status of irreducible necessities in the relationship of the individual to society. The creative surpluses are the vehicle of the inner identity which man calls his soul. No amount of success in practical adaptive ways can counterbalance the weight of the crushing depressions which come to the individual who has lost access to depth and vigor. Once a man has given away his heritage of a personal inner identity, there is no prescription which can cure the sickness that lack of enthusiasm brings, and no rewards so attractive that they can tame the antisocial tendencies released by a life lacking in inspiration.

In spite of the heavy penalty which men must pay for the loss of inner sensitivity and spontaneity, there is a tendency to turn aside from the search for these states of being. Men cannot pursue a significant search for an inner identity when they are overwhelmed by disorientation and disorganization. Enthusiasm must find a meaningful relationship with ideals, and inspiration requires opportunity which will not betray the best the individual has to offer. The greatest of all enthusiasms is love, and the highest inspirations come from the opportunities revealed by the operations of personal power. It is always difficult for love to identify that which is lovable and for power to find that which can be possessed, and when love must undergo disorientation because of intrusive sexuality, and power must experience disorganization because of unbridled celebration, the task of maintaining the growth of creative love and power becomes impossible.

Being in love always carries with it intangible longings for proximity to the loved object which must flow into sexualization. It can only become a secure and meaningful state when a power union accompanies it. Lovers belong to each other, and there is a vigilant possessiveness which must flow into celebration. The owning of another person at the surplus level can only be a free emotional state of value to the personality when a love union is also involved. In nature it is the female who is specialized to cement the love ties and the male who takes priority in the power union. The more submissive the female, the more the power capacities of the male are stirred, and reciprocally, the expanding dominance of the male deepens the love capacities of the female. This interaction is without fixed limits and enters the sexual and celebrative sphere as an inevitable progression in its own time and place. There is no need in the mated domain to sustain the kind of longing and vigilance which produces the state of being in love and needing to possess another person as it occurs in civilized personalities.

The developing capacity for idealization in the adolescent personality is vulnerable to the reaction of falling in love. Since idealization can only do its work when unalloyed with power, the sexualization of this love removes it from the area of self-development and halts the accompanying expansion of knowledge of the ideal. This creates a life of inner intensity which can become parasitic on the total personality.

The developing capacities for exploitation of the responsiveness of others in the adolescent personality are
vulnerable to invasion by the need for exclusive possession.
Since the discovery of resources can only find the necessary
freedom of exploration when it is not confined by love, the
invasion of power by celebration removes it from the area
of self-development and brings the accompanying expansion
of manipulative abilities to an end. This creates a life of
undirected energies which can undermine the constructiveness of the total personality.

THE MAGICAL AND THE MIRACULOUS

Love confers an expanding self-awareness which can only
lead to an expanding awareness of the world through idealization. If love is not to dissipate its constructive potential
in the kind of warmth and affection which encircles individuals in an emphathetic union of mutual feeling, shutting
out the world in the process, it must establish itself as a
working force in the affairs of men. The sensitivity which
is born of love can only find a creative outlet in analytic
thinking, the tool of the search for truth. Autonomous love
does not require that it be loved in turn. Love is fulfilled
by its capacity for self-maintenance. Love positions itself
in such a way that it can be the observer of anything that
exists in the world around it. The accumulation of knowledge and understanding through insight is the reward
sought by love. Love must participate in life in order to
expand what it sees, and the power elements utilized by
love are organized for adaptive purposes and are directed
toward maintaining that adaptation. The manipulative
aspects of creative love are not power organized but constitute the kind of work which serves the interests of the thing
loved. It is work divested of willfulness under the guidance

of faith, directed toward revealing the true nature of an ideal. Love arouses the creative thinking capacity of the civilized human being.

Personal power confers an expanding self-confidence which can only lead to meaningful involvements with the world through the exploitation of opportunity. If power is not to dissipate its constructive potential in the kind of vanity and pride which is cultivated by reciprocating helpfulness, ignoring the need to develop new resources, it must establish itself through loyalty and devotion, guided by a sense of integrity. The vigor which is born of personal power can only find an outlet through the inventive development of manipulative techniques, the vehicle of the search for the right. Autonomous power takes control and does not require that it be helped in return. Power is fulfilled by its capacity to survive in any situation. Power takes a stand in such a way that it can impress itself on any set of circumstances that come into existence in the world around it. The accumulation of ability and the capacity to take responsibility through mastery are the rewards sought by power. Power must submit to circumstances in order to expand its scope of participation in life, and the love elements utilized by power are oriented toward meeting adaptive needs and maintaining continuity in the adaptive life. The submissive aspects of creative power are not oriented toward a love goal, but rather provide the context in which the exploitation of opportunity occurs. It is characterized by devotion divested of self-consciousness under the influence of hope and is directed toward increasing the resources that exist in the world. Personal power awakens the constructive builder in the civilized human being.

Empathetic love can only expand when love is met by a response which is the mirror image of itself, and imitative power partnerships can only maintain an expanding spirit of cooperation when the individuals perform identical and interacting functions for each other. Empathetic love must be loved in turn; if it is not, the love cannot endure and hatred or withdrawal ensues. Imitative power must be possessed as well as possess others, and if the individual does not receive the help he expects, the power mood fails and anger or indifference ensues.

The more empathetic love excludes the world, the more readily it becomes sexual in nature. The more imitative power ignores external reality, the more readily it over-flows into celebrative channels. The physical aspects of empathetic love becomes essential to its maintenance, and the love relationship is no longer greater than the sexuality it breeds. The pursuit of casual enjoyment in imitative power becomes essential to its existence, and such power cannot contain the celebration it fosters.

An adequate sexuality requires that emphathetic moments exist in those relationships which become sexual, but the personality oriented by creative love is always capable of containing sexuality within the larger framework of the love capacities. The fulfillment of celebrative states requires episodes of shared mood elevation between individuals who join together for celebrative experience, but the personality organized by creative power is always capable of keeping celebration in a subsidiary relationship to the larger power capacities.

If thought processes can only exist when they are directly communicable, thinking must attain the status of insight as a necessary part of its existence. Such thinking abhors the unknown and is reinforced by empathetic sharing. If modes of action depend on the direct demonstrability of their effectiveness for their recognition, manipulative tech-niques must attain the status of mastery as a prerequisite for their existence. Such methods are intolerant of the chaotic and gain support by imitative identification.

When thinking capacities are used by a personality which cannot tolerate the privacy of creative analytic thought, the pressure of fear of the unknown creates a false passage into insight, utilizing magic as its route. Magic uses its own kind of authoritative knowledge and measures its effect through the sense of power it bestows on the thinker instead of through the revelation of the truth. Magic reaches a sense of power through its self-apparent communicability among all those who share its premises. When ideas accumulate power in the interpersonal relationships of the thinker himself, magical mechanisms are being used. Empathetic love is always vulnerable to magical thought since the need to be loved by others is an impelling one, and magic offers a way to arouse feeling without investment of psychological work and the growth processes which accompany it.

When the capacity for constructive manipulation is used by a personality which cannot tolerate the separateness of creative experimental action, the pressure of emerging rage at the chaotic leads to acceptance of a pseudo-mastery, utilizing a miraculous stance in the process. The usurpation of mastery by the miraculous employs an arbitrary view of the basis of effective behavior, and measures its effect in terms of its ability to influence others rather than on the establishment of the right. The miraculous always gives its agent a sense of group cohesion through its automatic demonstrability to all who accept involvement with it. When modes of action are organized to command love in interpersonal relationships, miraculous methods are being used. Imitative power is always vulnerable to the adoption of miraculous postures since the need to belong is an impelling one, and the miraculous offers a direct route to being important without the necessity of making enduring commitments and accepting the growth processes which they bring.

ADOLESCENT FANTASY AND PLAY-ACTING

The primitive empathetic feelings which are utilized magically give a sense of complete awareness without problems because idealization and its accompanying readiness for growth are excluded. Magical thinking enters the area of the occult, and those who share knowledge of the secret nature of things have a special access to communication. Magical depth of feeling avoids sexualization because the love it engenders is based on unobstructed warmth and closeness. It is therefore childlike in nature, and its existence depends on achieving a protected and withdrawn position, safe from the inroads of the problems which could expose its isolation from experience.

The elemental imitative attitudes which are used in miraculous behavior give a sense of lasting confidence in maintaining control, and this freedom from obstacles rests on the fact that the need to develop resources is excluded, thus dispensing with the need for psychological growth. Miraculous behavior enters the area of gregarious interactions, developing a gang spirit and laying the basis for mob psychology, and those who share the special capacities which the group identity confers can readily demonstrate their superiority. The miraculous posture avoids a celebrative overflow because the power it brings is based on unobstructed pride and automatic loyalty. Being childlike in nature, its existence depends on achieving a set of group beliefs which are not subject to question and which permit indifference to any other kind of principles, thus raising the individual above the level where social difficulties could expose his superficiality.

The adolescent in a state of growth finds himself alone and dissociated in relationship to the adult world of mature social roles. The more his honesty and courage bring him into conflict with the magical and miraculous elements in these roles, the more he finds himself cut off from the teaching and leadership functions he needs. The educational system is the natural place for his search for the help he needs. This system provides him with an opportunity to delay his assumption of full scale adult responsibilities, but a mere delay is not enough. If he uses higher education in a creative fashion, the real subject matter of his preoccupations and experimental probings reveals itself to be human nature itself. The more he is exposed to the unknown and chaotic in himself and others, the greater is the fear and rage he must comprehend and control, and for this task he needs intellectual and methodological tools which are free of magical and miraculous qualities.

In the finding of mental health and social harmony in the unknown and chaotic world of the creative adolescent, fantasy and play-acting loom large as assets of the personality. Fantasy permits the discovery of new facets of the self-awareness in relationship to imagined experience, without committing the individual to the mobility which would be required to bring an expanding experience into his life. Fantasy permits self-development without loss of the protected status which withdrawal confers. As long as fantasy is part of the growth structure of the personality, it remains a healthy phenomenon, but when it becomes a tool for preparing the self for adaptive action, it encourages the intrusion of creative elements where they do not belong, and results in an overinvestment of feeling in practical matters.

Play-acting permits the emergence within the self of new aspects of self-confidence in relationship to pretended circumstances, without committing the individual to the selective exploration which would be required if he were to expand the scope of his opportunities. Play-acting permits self-development without responsibility for the maintenance of continuity, under the influence of indifference. As long as the play-acting is part of the growth structure of the personality, it does not interfere with the development of basic social conformity, but when it becomes intrusive on adaptive behavior it builds energies which cannot find socially acceptable outlets.

Fantasy cultivates depth and sensitivity in circumstances where the inner identity would otherwise be lost, thus conferring an essential continuity upon the self-awareness. Fantasy is highly selective, being guided by pleasure alone, and it cannot accept the kind of involvement in service to an ideal which problem solving thinking entails. Where the self-awareness is primarily carried in the form of fantasy, the degree of withdrawal may be very great. To overcome this withdrawal, the adolescent attempts to communicate with others on a basis of a shared fantasy life. As long as the pleasure-seeking quality of fantasy remains apparent, such empathetic sharing does not invade the realm of analytic thinking. When the individual sees the world around him as if it were a product of his own fantasy, and communicates his view of it to others as a form of insight, he is in the presence of magical thinking. The structure of magic is such as to preserve the continuity of pleasure while permitting a relationship with experience. In magical thinking, concepts are invaded by willfulness, and the individual comprehends nothing which disturbs the sense of access to truth.

Play-acting cultivates vigor and spontaneity in circumstances where the inner identity could not otherwise be expressed, thus providing for an essential integrity which preserves self-confidence. Play-acting requires a high degree of mobility, being guided by enjoyment alone, and it cannot accept the kind of commitment to the development of resources which the constructive overcoming of obstacles entails. Where the self-confidence is carried primarily in the form of play-acting, the amount of indifference may be very great. To overcome this lack of feelingfulness, the adolescent attempts to form mutual identifications on the basis of cooperative play-acting activities. As long as the goal remains within the scope of shared enjoyment, there is no invasion of the area belonging to the experimental development of skills. When the individual deals with the world around him as a playground which exists for the exercise of egotistical self-display, sharing his modes of manipulating it with others as a form of mastery, he is in the presence of the miraculous. The structure of the miraculous is such as to preserve the uncompromising nature of enjoyment through an inherent freedom from opposition, while at the same time attaining a sense of involvement with the environment. In miraculous activity modalities of constructive action are invaded by an inappropriate self-awareness, and the individual preserves his spontaneity by dealing with nothing which would disturb the conviction that his behavior is an inevitable expression of the right.

THE SEARCH FOR NORMALCY

The adolescent has a heightened sense of being different from others since the autonomous search for individuality takes up so much of the psychic life. At the same time the need to deal with fear of the unknown and rage at the provocation inherent in the chaotic leads the individual to social empathy and identifications within the adolescent community which reach extreme forms of expression. The individual welcomes empathetic warmth from his own kind, becoming vulnerable to great intensities in love feelings toward whatever mirrors his own nature. There are also extravagant mutual identifications among those who support each other's pride, leading to reinforcement of the power posture wherever the unity of youth can make common cause against conventional ways. Magical and

miraculous mechanisms may be utilized in holding the
adolescent community together, especially so that emerging sex and celebration may be contained within a larger
context, but if the personality is to grow it cannot avoid
independent development of the insights and mastery which
delegate magic and miracles to a childish past. Growth requires that the autonomous part of the self meet the impact
of sex and celebration. As the individual deals with this
challenge, he is only more alone and more separate in his
relationship with the adult community, and his creative
reachings among his own kind bring him to an unavoidable
confrontation with the idealizing and exploiting aspects
of his nature.

 No individual who grows up in the civilized world is
really prepared to understand or deal with the extremes
of his own submissive or dominant tendencies as they are
released by the interpersonal interactions which lie outside the orderly world of family life and the social roles
it sponsors. If the individual accepts the pathway to personal
development which dependence on familial influence provides, his social maturation may be a fairly simple and
direct matter of following in the footsteps of the parent
of the same sex. In this case his independent idealizing and
exploiting capacities must be left in an undeveloped form
since their intrusion on familial empathy and identification
can only interfere with these mechanisms. If the father's
masculine role is taken to be worthy of idealization, and
the mother's feminine role is accepted as a model of altruistic
surrender, without regard to the full psychological dimensions of assertive or yielding character identity, the adolescent cannot deviate from his dependence on familial beliefs
and established ways except at the cost of disillusionment
and humiliation. Disillusioned love leads to hatred, and
humiliated power exposes the self to anger. The hunger of
the yielding personality for an ideal cannot be satisfied by

idealizing the self or extensions of the self, no matter how much the parental model may be in advance of the self in establishing a mature social adjustment. This kind of pseudo-idealization reduces personality development to a matter of enduring the passage of time until the evolution of the career identity has accumulated the necessary access to power. The high purposes which the assertive personality can bring to accomplishment only through the finding of exploitable resources cannot be fulfilled by utilizing the level of responsiveness of which he himself is capable, or which he finds in his own familial environment, even though the greater maturity of his parental model provides him with an example of submissiveness which serves the interests of social conformity. This kind of identification confines the individual to a limited arena of action in which the personality development becomes a matter of waiting for the necessary attachments and loyalties to emerge from his gregarious activities. His search for greater self-realization proceeds without genuine control of his own destiny. He becomes the victim of circumstances, looking always for a gift of good fortune from life circumstances.

The relationship between the sexes is the carrier of the image of psychological normalcy in the civilized world. To establish a relationship with the opposite sex to the extent that it involves the sexual and celebrative life is taken to be the essential basic element in growing up to be like other people. Heterosexual relationships are counted on to tame the unbridled power strivings of the developing assertive personality and to overcome the sensitive shyness of the developing yielding personality. Heterosexuality functions as a source of psychological balance through drawing individuals into social roles which they do not have to find for themselves.

The mated interaction between the sexes in nature utilizes balance in a different fashion. The masculinity of the male and the femininity of the female come to their fullest expression in the courtship. The mating provides for a partial subjection of the male and a partial dominance of the female through the inherent balance provided by sexual and celebrative mechanisms. The male is brought into a feminizing tension bearing state through sexual excitement but this is limited in time by the orgastic goal. The female is aroused to a masculinizing energy accumulation through the elevated celebrative mood but this is focused in a circumscribed area through the altruistic surrender to the male. The price of balance which the male and female attain is the formation of the domain in which the pair become a permanent, complete, and autonomous unit in relationship to their world.

The establishment of an inner identity is antecedent to the emergence of a heterosexual adjustment in human beings. Any personality which is formed by a sexualized and celebrative union with a person of the opposite sex can have no inner identity, but only succeeds in establishing a dream-like and pretentious imitation of masculine or feminine traits as they occur in nature. When men attempt to find a personality this way, there is no genuine individuality in it, and their only recourse for self-expression lies in the direction of a competitive struggle with other men which has no constructive aspects, with the female differentiating herself by attaching herself to the victor.

The standards of normalcy are established by a consensus of opinion as to what normalcy is to be. The meaning and value of the concept of normalcy in the life of the community can only be discovered in those contexts where it is used to reinforce the stability of the social roles. Once the individual moves out of the adaptive area into an independent search for truth and right in human affairs, normalcy ceases to confer any usable identity on the individual. In the same way that the growing individual must learn to make an investment in adaptive maturity which is limited to its practical function, he learns to limit the influence of the concept of normalcy to those contexts where it is appropriate. Without a private and separate life where the inner identity can find its own development, the individual becomes a prisoner of normalcy and the victim of the loss of growth capacity which accompanies it. His inner identity and his social identity become the same thing, and privacy and separateness confer no psychological rewards.

THE BASIS OF PSYCHOLOGICAL INDEPENDENCE

Once the images and patterns of normalcy are laid aside in contexts where the individual is psychologically on his own, the growing personality must find its own continuity and integrity. Men call on knowledge of themselves in order to retain their inner security and mental health in the face of the crises which growth brings, and they must utilize established instrumentalities of self-control in order to retain their inner freedom and social harmony in the process of growth. If their faith in human understanding and their hopeful expectation of fulfillment for human responsibility fail, there is no way they can continue on the path of growth alone, and they must then take as direct a route as possible into an all-encompassing conformity, without autonomous selectivity or mobility. Individuals who make such a settlement find themselves cheated of the peace of mind and spontaneity in living which they expected to attain. Although they live by the superficial social standards which are generally recognized to characterize conformity and a sense of duty, the real essence of goodness and beauty has departed from their lives.

Psychological independence requires a basic faith and hopefulness which cannot be destroyed by the vicissitudes of growth. If the meaning of love in the life of mankind is understood, the individual can accept the periods of relative emotional emptiness which analytic thinking in human affairs requires. The sense of inferiority which comes from the failures of wisdom brings the personality to the brink of an alienation from the environment. This kind of aloneness must come to a personality which is prepared to accept privacy if the process of developing new truth is to go forward. If the value of personal power in inter-personal relationships has molded the character of men in a way that can be demonstrated to others, the individual can accept those situations where experimental human in-volvements bring temporary aimlessness and ineffectuality. The sense of guilt which comes from the inadequacies of strength brings the personality to the edge of emotional impoverishment. This kind of dissociation from the world of human rewards must come to a personality which has the means of accepting separateness if the development of new modalities of the right is to proceed.

The need for love can flow in either empathetic or creative channels. The biological and social helplessness of the infant and child requires the maintenance of a nurturing love as a source of security in the face of threats to the basic continuity of warmth and affection in its interaction with the world. The maintenance of a basic level of co-hesiveness with humanity draws heavily on this kind of empathetic love. Empathetic loves gives what it wants to get and must receive what it gives. If obstructions of a serious nature exist such love turns to hate and seeks to effect a withdrawal. Idealizing or creative love rests on faith and brings new understanding into being. It draws its motivation for giving from the inherent imbalance in its nature. Idealiz-ing love does not predicate its existence on what it gets, but accepts the challenge of maintaining the permanence of its influence as a task which belongs to its essential identity. It is vulnerable to imbalance and to the loss of inner unity which leads to neurotic and psychotic phenomena. Either kind of love can become sexualized. In the mated mechanisms of nature it is the non-empathetic type of love which is the repository of sexualization. When empathetic love is sexualized the sexuality tends to overwhelm love itself and its natural boundaries are eliminated, leading to perverse manifestations. Much of civilized sexuality is psychologically perverse, and the boundaries which contain and guide it are established by social convention, so that the definition of perversity has become a social rather than a psychological matter.

The assumption of personal power is motivated by two aspects of the need for dominance, expressing itself either through identification or exploitation. The sense of attachment in the infant and child to a protecting power operates as a source of freedom which preserves a basic self-confidence, maintaining poise in the face of frustrations. The maintenance of a sense of belonging in social life is fed by the gregarious group spirit arising from shared identifications. Imitative power does not ask an existence separate from its reinforcing partnerships. The fraternal sharing obliterates any need to give without receiving, and the presence of obstructions in cooperative relationships leads to anger and subsequent indifference. The creative form of power develops the resources it exploits, using hope as its operating principle, and thereby expands the scope of personal responsibility. It draws its motivation for giving from the inherent imbalance of its nature. Such power does not find its expression through the reinforcement of the cooperation it receives from others, but accepts the function of maintaining the integrity of its individual influence as an inherent aspect of its identity. It is vulnerable to a loss of inner continuity which becomes the basis of delinquency and major psychotic mood disturbances. Either kind of power

can overflow into celebrative channels. In the mated mechanisms of nature it is exploitative power which establishes
the domain and makes a place for celebrative phenomena.
When imitative power becomes celebrative, the celebrative
expression tends to overwhelm the integrity of power and
celebration expands out of context, leading to addiction
phenomena. Much of personal power in the civilized world
is psychologically addicted, and the boundaries which contain and guide it are established by social custom, so that
addiction takes on a social rather than a psychological meaning.

The emergence of the creative spirit in human beings
infuses their lives with a sense of greatness of inner purpose
which once attained cannot be lightly laid aside. Men can
adjust themselves to psychological emptiness and impoverishment only when they have not known anything else. Once
they have undertaken the labors of love, or pledged themselves to the loyalties arising from power, they can withdraw
or become indifferent only at the peril of their existence as
human beings. To preserve access to the best in themselves,
men will risk their lives and bring all their worldly adaptive
accomplishments into jeopardy. For such men, survival without their creative identity ceases to be survival at all. Those
who have found maturity by excluding creative imbalance
from their lives make normalcy the goal of human existence
and look on their creative fellow beings as deviant, alien,
and even dangerous to the stability of society.

PATTERNS OF NORMALCY

Whenever the mature social roles dominate the psychological existence of men to the exclusion of the creative spirit,
custom and convention must establish the basis of human
understanding and responsibility. The socially formed patterns of normalcy replace the individual's search for truth

and right. Since being normal becomes the test of the adequacy of a mature adjustment, it becomes essential that no serious problems or obstacles be allowed to develop in the image or operational effectiveness of being a normal person. Anything in the view of life and way of life which does not serve the purposes of normalcy must be ignored and neglected. A substantial part of man's psychological life becomes secret and dissociated as a result. This is not the same kind of privacy and separateness which characterizes the creative process because it is a permanent and fixed state of affairs. The most notable area in which the secret and the dissociated operate when maturity usurps the functions of growth is in the sexual and celebrative sphere. The image of sexual normalcy is constructed out of elements which favor family stability and whatever does not fit is taken to be unworthy of human awareness. The resulting general ignorance is given a wide social support. Sexual deviation is not actually taken to be abnormal in itself, but only the exposure of it in a way that challenges the general agreement to ignore it. Normal celebrative behavior is also channeled by the need to protect family stability, and whatever emerges outside this context is allowed to run its course as an isolated phenomenon which is accepted as a product of human weakness beyond the range of human control. Celebrative deviation is not necessarily considered abnormal in itself, but the acceptance of it as a worthy part of the psychological life is what marks the individual as abnormal. The ultimate identity which normalcy achieves is one of dogmatic beliefs and autocratic conformity, and the depressive impact of this kind of social identity is relieved by an admixture with an indulgent acceptance of superficiality and a permissive tolerance of weakness. The human character is taken to be inevitably selfish and vain, and anyone who cannot accept his fellows in such a context is barred from full empathy and identification with them.

Any creative expansion of human truth has revolutionary implications in the interpersonal relationships of civilized man. The way men see each other's natures, and the way they communicate about it, cannot be confined to being a mere intellectual exercise, nor can such preoccupations readily find a protected place in which they can develop as a body of scientific insights. Any significant expansion of psychological awareness brings social ideas into question, and this process constitutes a threat to the image of normalcy in human affairs. It is not possible to have one definition of normalcy for social purposes, and another one which is psychologically true in a scientific sense. Any divergence between them creates serious stresses within the personality of the thinker, and he can pursue the course of truth seeking only at his peril. When the social adequacy of the mature individual requires him to ignore the psychologically perverse nature of socially accepted patterns of feeling, he is barred from the kind of honesty on which truth seeking in human affairs is based. If he exposes himself to an unlimited questioning of social beliefs, there is no way to tell how far the resulting upheaval in his personal adjustment will go, and he will have no guarantee that he can replace these beliefs with something better. It is because of the existence of this barrier to awareness that the science of human nature has lagged so far behind the development of other scientific disciplines.

Any creative expansion of the right in the direction of higher moral standards brings civilized man to a heretical rejection of established principles in interpersonal relationships. The aspects of human behavior with which men choose to become involved, and the degree to which they accept responsibility for what they do or fail to do, cannot be left to the operation of chance or fate, but their devotion to group undertakings has lacked the atmosphere of permanency which permits objective development of an engineering type of mastery. Any significant expansion of individual control threatens the hegemony of social institutions. It is not possible to have one standard for normalcy in conventional social activities and another one which is recognized to be right when morality and justice are in the focus of attention. Morality is only another name for mastery which takes cognizance of the full range of human reality. Any divergence between the standards of behavior of conventional normalcy and what is psychologically right creates serious stresses in the personality of the man of action, and he can pursue the course of individual responsibility only if he is willing to pay the price. When social adequacy requires a tolerance of addicted outlets for power impulses, justifying such outlets as inevitable and natural, the individual is barred from the kind of personal courage on which the reaching for the right is based. If he departs from the established patterns of social identification, there is no way to predict how isolated he will become, and there is no guarantee that he can find new avenues of interaction which will be better. It is because of this barrier against bringing personal responsibility into the area of human control that the objective development of mastery techniques has lagged so far behind the development of engineering skills in the non-human fields.

SIN AND EVIL

Love is an end in itself when it exists in a context created by power. When sexuality emerges in this context, it does the work of love and is contained by it. The kind of empathetic love which responds to a reflection of itself can only give to another on a basis of what is given in return, and such love can never be its own end. The sexuality which appears in empathetic love tends to overflow in a promiscuous fashion and cannot be contained except by prohibitions.

The mutual indulgence of empathetic love stirs all the appetites, including sexual desire, and may succeed in ignoring its selfish status because it makes a place for the selfishness of another. Once appetites have been gratified, there is a tendency for shame to take over, and this state of flatness of affect may lead to the cultivation of more appetite. Any need which takes hold in this fashion has a perverse structure.

Power is an end in itself when it takes its being in a context created by love. When celebration emerges in this context, it constitutes a response to the commitments of power and is contained by it. The kind of imitative power which is reinforced by the cooperation of identical partners can only give to others on the basis of what it gets, and such power can never be an end in itself. The celebration which appears in imitative power tends to overflow in an undisciplined fashion and cannot be contained except by the control of authority. The mutual permissiveness of imitative power awakens purposefulness in any direction that promises enjoyment, including the celebrative outlets, and may succeed in camouflaging its vanity because it takes its being in an atmosphere of deference to the vanity of another. Once the purposes aroused by imitative power have accomplished their ends, there is a tendency for guilt to take over, and this state of mood depression may lead to a reactive striving toward freedom from restraint. When the individual's strivings are organized in this cyclical fashion, the mechanism of addiction has taken hold.

Both perversity and addiction have a necessary place in the psychological life of civilized man. There are elements in a mature psychological adjustment which depend on the cultivation of empathetic love and imitative power for their expression. If sex and celebration are to be incorporated into family life, mated mechanisms must be replaced by familial indulgence and permissiveness. The problem with empathetic love lies in the fact that its perverse structure is hidden from the individual. The understanding of sexuality in general becomes distorted, putting a serious barrier in the path of the growth of the love capacities. Love cannot grow if it is not in a position to deal with the sexual component which is stirred by the growth of idealizing love. If such sexuality is alien to the personality, the individual may be forced to turn away from psychological growth altogether.

The difficulty with imitative celebration lies in the fact that it brings behavior into being which must remain outside the reach of rational personal responsibility. The capacity for self-control in celebrative matters in general is compromised, and this reduces access to growth of the power capacities. The individual must be able to deal with the celebrative moods released by the reachings of exploitative power. If such celebrative attitudes are disorganizing to the personality, the individual may be required to turn away from growth altogether.

What civilized man has done to aid himself in keeping empathetic sexuality in its place is to develop the concept of sin, putting the mark of socially reinforced shame on sexual passion which tends to emerge outside of the prescribed patterns of feeling. The more threatening sexuality is to the continuity of family feeling, the greater the sinfulness is taken to be, and therefore incest is the most dangerous. The individual also maintains control over imitative celebration through the elaboration of a strict code of behavior which brings guilt to those untrammeled celebrative impulses which are taken to be unnatural and based on evil intentions. The more threatening celebrative attitudes are to family unity, the more evil their sources are taken to be, and the leading astray of family members is most to be condemned.

The farther men get from independent access to creative

love and power, the more they come to believe that their real natures contain a sinful and evil core which only arbitrary law and autocratic authority can contain. In periods of renaissance of the human spirit, men challenge the dishonesty of sexual ignorance and put aside the cowardice which maintains the established neglect of the celebrative tendencies. In so doing, they pass through a stage of rejection of the limitations which keep sexual indulgence and celebrative permissiveness within bounds. They begin to recognize the nature of perversity and begin to deal with addictive behavior in a rational and objective way. If this expansion in the scope of human awareness and control is not to overwhelm the ideas and institutions which are basic to maturity, it must rest on genuine insights and mastery and not deteriorate into a cynical and opportunistic acceptance of undifferentiated sex and celebration. Men cannot throw off their ancient burden of sin and evil without the inner growth which permits them to substitute autonomous access to unselfish love and to power of high moral standards.

The removal of the restraints imposed by arbitrary law and autocratic authority brings transitional phases of disorientation and disorganization which opens the door to unhealthy and antisocial phenomena. As men refuse to be limited by the inner conviction that they are sinful, and throw off the supervision of authority which assumes they are evil, much evidence will accumulate of their sinful and evil natures. Only idealism can find the true development that is taking place, and only the sense of reality which reaches for new human resources can be trusted to discover the right basis of human morality.

The development of a science of human nature depends on insights into the nature of the disorientation and disorganization which accompany the removal of social restraints. The new awareness of sexuality which Freud

brought to mankind was accompanied by a cynical acceptance of the influence of sin and evil on the structure of
the personality. Freud identified disorientation and disorganization as an established and continuing component
of psychological life. In so doing, he failed to comprehend
the creative resources of civilized man. The Freudian id
is a dream-like concept of a hidden well of fragments of
sensual greed and unbridled violent impulses, beyond the
reach of reason and without direction. The id was equated
with basic biological instinctual tendencies, but where this
kind of phenomenon exists in nature would be impossible
to say. The only place it really exists is in the world of
rebellion against the false idealization of aggressive authority which gave birth to Freud's psychological system.

IDEALISM AND THE SENSE OF REALITY

Idealizing love and exploitative power cannot be successfully used to build family life because the kind of inner
growth which they bring does not fit the stable adaptive
goals of the family. It is also true that the successful family
is a homogenous one in which the similar character specialization of the parents creates the necessary background for
the character development of the children. The elimination
of the fundamental mated relationship which builds the
domain in nature means that the personality comes to
marriage with its inner identity already established and
with its sexual and celebrative capacities fully developed
and ready to be expressed.

Part of the psychological task of reaching maturity in
the civilized world consists in learning to make a place for
perverse and addictive tendencies in certain interpersonal
contexts. These tendencies are limited and controlled in
early adolescence while the individual is still dependent
on his family. Without prohibitions and active supervision

such outlets tend to overwhelm the personality, disturbing
the growing capacities for creative thinking and constructive
action. There are no natural limits on perversity and addiction. The general tendency of the rebellious and heretical
adolescent to throw off sexual rules and celebrative restraint
cannot succeed because of the inner disturbances which
are produced by such false methods of self-realization. What
the creative strivings of the adolescent require is that he
find understanding of that part of himself which has the
impure coloration of perversity and that he gain the capacity
for personal responsibility in dealing with that aspect of his
activities which has the artificial quality of addiction. There
can be no ultimate objection to making a place for the
selfish and the egotistical in human social life, but when
these tendencies intrude into the place which belongs to
the work of love and the constructive commitments of power,
the individual is robbed of his inner autonomy. As the
growing personality learns to keep perverse and addictive
tendencies within the prescribed boundaries, the individual
becomes more capable of investing the rest of himself in the
kind of personal search which brings the creative faculties
into being.

It is the prerogative of youth to reject the corruption and
injustice which infiltrates the mature social adaptations of
civilized man. The more society as a whole is in a state of
renaissance, the more this rejection is an essential part of
psychological growth. The truth seeker cannot avoid exposing the problems which dishonesty has kept hidden. The
individual who builds new modalities of the right cannot
bypass the social distress areas which cowardice has ignored.
When the adolescent comes to a full awareness of the corrupt
elements in mature adaptation and begins to challenge the
injustice which is part of conventional social adequacy, he
finds his inner equilibrium threatened by a rebellious
hatred and a heretical anger. Unless he can find an ideal

worthy of the depth of feeling his enthusiasm brings, and a sense of reality of sufficient scope to utilize the inspiration which his vigor releases, his rebellious behavior and his heretical thinking will become ends in themselves.

Rebellion and heresy do not provide the individual with guidance in the face of his own perverse and addictive tendencies. The personality cannot win understanding of perversity by a rebellious emersion in it, even though such defiance brings new sophistication through the changing of the rules laid down by the previous generation. All that can emerge from this psychological event is a new set of rules which open the door to new indulgences, but it cannot alter the fundamental lack of genuine insight into the nature of perversity itself. Neither can the personality attain a capacity for self-mastery in the area of addiction by a heretical acceptance of all opportunities for personal freedom, even though such willfulness brings new ways to escape from the control of authority. All that the individual can find is a new system of authoritative control, and although it provides new avenues of self-expression, it cannot make up for the fundamental lack of enduring modalities of mastery over addiction itself.

Love which responds to love and power which associates itself with power are essential to the kind of stable equilibrium which social maturity requires. Within the encirclement of warmth-giving love, men find balance through the dutiful services which they perform for each other. United by the shared pride which power brings, men find balance through the loyal attachments which they form for each other. In such a stable world socially reinforced and controlled perversity and addiction cease to be recognizable as such. It is only when the idealizing faculties are fully engaged that the individual is forced to become aware of the presence of perverse mechanisms in family life. When an expanding sense of reality has fully engaged the power seeking faculties of the individual, he is forced to deal with the addictive mechanisms which are part of family life. Because of the resulting tendency to reduce involvement in familial gratifications and accomplishments, the development of the creative capacities may appear to threaten family stability. There is no ultimate reason, however, why the creative individual cannot make a place within himself for all the psychological elements which family life requires, provided that he retains the autonomous capacity to search for truth and right in the appropriate interpersonal contexts. If the family attempts to support its stability by representing itself to be the outlet for the best in human nature, it can only end in opposing the creative growth of its members.

AUTONOMY AND THE SURPLUSES

The creative inner identity comes out of the specialization of the character in either a yielding or assertive pattern, and this specialization is found and maintained through an independent relationship with society in general. Familial relationships and the conventional social roles tend to obliterate the clear focus of character specialization. Although the individual utilizes his character specialization in the adaptive relationships of maturity, these relationships do not encourage the further growth of his autonomous individuality. The individual who is creative in interpersonal relationships must find continuity and integrity for his inner self in contexts which are favorable for it and he cannot do this unless his love of mankind leads to involvement with other people, and his personal power status develops genuine attachments in human situations. The involvements of love are for the sake of love, and the attachments of power gratify the nature of power. When individuals have the inner security and freedom to make such relationships, they employ their selectivity and mobility to reach society in general through a series of particular relationships which come and go throughout a lifetime, the choice of such relationships depending on the rate of growth of the self and the human contexts which are accessible. The relationships express and reinforce the inner identity in a way to bring out the best in the self, calling on wisdom and strength to the fullest dimensions the individual can attain at that particular time. Such relationships are included in the general category of friendships.

The idealization of others needs a masculine ideal for its growth and expression. Without a meaningful capacity for interaction with individuals who embody genuine masculinity, love remains withdrawn, autistic, and theoretical. The development of human resources through creative exploitation requires an expanding sense of reality. Feminine responsiveness alone can give the necessary opportunity for the growth and expression of the power capacities. Without relationships with feminine psychological elements of value to the self, power remains indifferent, euphoric, and artificial.

Love which exists for its own sake can only reach the vividness of an experiential world in the presence of power which exists for itself, and power which is its own end can only find the overflowing abundance of resources which brings genuine richness of opportunity in the presence of self-sustaining love. This interaction between the love and power surpluses is exactly the same psychological phenomenon which creates the mated domain in nature. Idealizing love must attain desexualization if it is to do its work in the world, but the personality must not be desexualized in the process. The depth of the self which idealizing love brings into being remains the real source of sexuality in civilized human beings. This sexuality constitutes a reservoir of deep feelingfulness, ready to seek sexual excitement and orgastic discharge for its own sake. It may involve the individual in sexual relationships with others or take autoerotic channels, depending on the special conditions of its emergence. Man is the only animal who makes an adaptation to his own sexuality, choosing a sex life in the context of a growing interpersonal involvement with his fellow men. Because he chooses sexuality under appropriate conditions it does not overflow into any and every channel which love creates. His sexual life acts as a catalyst to his love capacities. When he is familiar with his own sexuality he is able to deal with sexual feeling in the course of loving others. If his sexual nature remains unfamiliar and alien, the threat of its emergence will stand athwart the path of the growth of love.

Power which discovers an expanding reality must not overflow indiscriminately into celebration if it is to develop the necessary loyalties. The barrier against celebration must not result in a loss of access to celebrative experience within the personality. The vigor and spontaneity which exploitative power brings into being is the real source of the civilized celebrative capacities. The celebrative tendencies create a potential for total surrender to enjoyable activities for their own sake, either in following the impulses of the moment or in interacting with the celebrative tendencies of others. Man is the only animal who must make a personal adjustment to his own celebrative capacities, selecting patterns of celebrative expression in the context of a growing interpersonal involvement with others. Because man chooses the areas and patterns of his celebrative release, celebration does not overflow indiscriminately into all the channels that power creates. The celebrative life acts as a catalyst to the power capacities. When the individual has established modalities of control in dealing with the celebrative tendencies, he can accept a heightened mood in his power interactions with others without losing his capacity for self-control. If his celebrative nature remains outside the scope of his capacity to take responsibility for himself, the threat of its intrusion on his adaptive life will erect a barrier against the growth of power.

Friendship is the repository of the surplus interpersonal life. It is the psychological proving ground of the love capacities, seeking always to find the conditions where love may deepen without the necessity of sexual overflow, in the service of the growth of the self and of those who share its psychological needs. Friendship is the workshop of the power capacities, reaching always for those circumstances where power may find spontaneity of expression without the necessity of celebrative overflow, in the service of the growth of the self and of those who make common cause with its psychological goals.

FRIENDSHIP AND CREATIVITY

Once men have established an inner identity they cannot give it up without exposing themselves to emotional flatness and depression of mood. The transition into autonomous enthusiasm and inspiration in the view of life and way of life is through a one way door. Some men do not either seek or find that passage, preferring the safe territory of a maturity which clings to balance as the first psychological law of life. In that territory human problems and obstacles are not allowed to exist unless the individual is overwhelmed by them, and when this crisis point has been reached it is too late to find the necessary insights and mastery for a creative solution. What some men consider full emotional gratifications other men reject as bovine insensibility, and the activities which bring a sense of accomplishment to some are only a form of futility to others. Neither can live in the other's world. A sudden influx of personal depth and vigor in a life guided by dogmatic and autocratic maturity can only lead to a disastrous loss of social empathy and identification, whereas the individual who turns his back on the best in himself after it has come into focus in his life must pass through the valley of the shadow of death and through a wasteland of impoverishment.

Social progress in human matters depends on the number of people having access to an autonomous identity within themselves. A world which ignores human problems and bypasses human obstacles cannot expect to find the necessary insights and mastery when crises threaten the stable equilibrium of society. At such times men think and act on an emergency basis, impelled by fear and rage, and are capable of the greatest hostility and destructiveness toward each other. It is the emergence of these crises which teaches men that in spite of the many social accomplishments of civilized human beings, they have yet to attain a genuine maturity in interpersonal relationships. Society itself is adolescent in psychological structure. Those who cannot recognize this fact believe that civilization creates a social veneer beneath which men are inherently hostile and destructive.

Friendship provides the ideals and resources for psychological growth. Although the goals of friendship are creative, and in this sense are neither sexual or celebrative, the scope of friendship can accept no limitations in its awareness of sexuality nor in its capacity to deal with celebrative phenomena. Friendship cannot flourish in the presence of the secret and the separate within its own contexts. Creative interpersonal relationships are not bound by the beliefs and modes of behavior which men take for granted in establishing the social roles of their mature adaptive life. If the specialization of the personality is to survive the pressure toward a balanced psychological existence, the individual must find interpersonal relationships in which self-development and self-expression are of primary importance, and such relationships become the real source of inner security and freedom. These relationships are forged by individuals out of their own psychological needs and purposes, and the less they are influenced by the stable social roles the more they can perform the psychological function for which they are intended.

When love and power find their proper developmental ground in the selective and mobile world which friendship brings into being, these forces must face a difficult struggle with unattached sexuality and the undirected celebrative energies. Men must learn to deal with the pressure for expression of these biological surpluses in an interpersonal world where love accepts no limit and power has no established boundaries. The social roles assign the expression of sex and celebration to the relationships of men and women. This seems to be entirely natural since it follows the biological instinct patterns. In the civilized world, the development of love through idealization and of power through exploitation brings sexual and celebrative phenomena into being which have no necessary relationship to the union of male and female. If the creative capacities are invested where they do not belong, in an attempt to capture all sexual and celebrative phenomena for the union of male and female, there is a resultant development of stresses in the relationships between the sexes, upsetting the balance, equanimity, and stability which belongs to family life. At the same time the continuity and integrity of the creative inner identity deteriorates.

Because of the gender differentiations which are carried by the social roles, in which surface social and personal characteristics are seen as the real carriers of masculine or feminine identity, the relationships of men and women are generally not available to friendship for the working through of the maxium potentials of depth and vigor. The encouragement of socially established channels of pleasure and enjoyment is taken to be the proper grounds on which men and women come together, and if their interactions find tendencies which are psychologically important, the relationship is guided into the social institution of marriage. Love and power relationships outside marriage between men and women readily overflow into promiscuous sexuality and transient celebrative partnerships. Such sex and celebration is only apparently mated in pattern, utilizing reinforcement of the surface gender characteristics. Sex is often found without relationship to celebrative outlets, and this kind of sexuality is highly empathetic, leading to mutual withdrawal, a high level of secrecy, and a sense of shame. Conversely, celebration may bring temporary partnerships without relationship to sexual experience, releasing a heightened mood and unrestrained identification. Such relationships are characterized by shared indifference toward others with dissociation and subsequent guilt.

Because of the readiness of sexual and celebrative overflow between the sexes, it is in the area of the fraternal relationships of men that the proving ground of friendship takes its being. There is no inherent biological or psychological reason why this exclusion of women should be inevitable, but there are strong social reasons for it. This exclusion underlies the historical depreciation of women in civilized society, and forms the basis of the ongoing conflict between men and women which becomes intensified in times of rapid social change.

HOMOSEXUALITY AND CELEBRATIVE PARTNERSHIPS

As men detach themselves from their social roles and turn toward a fuller participation in those interpersonal relationships which fulfill their inner identities, they must call upon their independent understanding of human nature and their capacity for responsibility in unstructured human interactions. At such times they release new feelings and attitudes. The self-awareness which is kept hidden in their social roles, and the self-confidence which is kept dissociated in similar circumstances, manifest themselves without restriction in interpersonal relationships, utilizing a full access to personal honesty and courage. Without the unalloyed honesty which is communicated within the framework of friendship, and without the uncompromising willingness to become involved in any aspect of human reality, friendship is divested of its potential for psychological growth and becomes merely an extension of the fraternal familial bond. Creative friendship is based on communicated truth, and the identification with the right which the other embodies. Out of such interactions friends use each other and respect each other's identity, using the parts of their psychological natures which are above and beyond the commitments of daily adaptive living.

When one member of a pair is yielding in his psychological specialization and the other is assertive, and each brings an imbalance within himself to the relationship, there is a major expansion in the scope of their cohesion and interaction, bringing new opportunities for personal growth and an accompanying readiness to face the unknown and the chaotic in the human world. Just as the creative search for truth and right utilizes mechanisms which are rooted in the mated relationships found in nature, so do growth relationships between men of opposite character utilize the kind of interacting reinforcement of inner identity which characterizes the mated domain. These mechanisms are powerful in their influence on the lives of men. They bring inner security and freedom into being which once experienced will not be willingly relinquished.

Friendship is inherently intolerant of the secret and separate in its own relationships. The closeness of friendship leads to a pure kind of communication in which words are used to reveal thoughts, not to conceal them. The whole superficial panoply of the social roles drops away, bringing the peace of mind which only mutual acceptance on a basis of a merciless self-exposure can make possible. Because friendship follows no established standards in permitting interpersonal involvement, it leads to a special readiness for accepting behavioral individuality, in which modes of behavior express what the individual really wants to do, not what he is pretending he is. As the social roles are laid aside, a spontaneity emerges which only cooperation on a basis of shared untrammeled individuality can release.

The personal honesty and courage of friendship is receptive to knowledge of sexuality and accepts the obligation of dealing with the phenomena which celebration brings into being. The high levels of empathy which shared sexual awareness brings make it possible that the relationship itself may be sexualized. If this is not to happen, it is because men choose that it should not, rather than finding it outside the boundaries of the possible. When the barriers against sexuality which come from the same sources as familial incest prohibitions are extended to the entire range of non-marital interpersonal relationships, there is a loss of capacity for self-exposure and a limitation in the depth that can be reached.

The high levels of identification which acceptance of celebrative phenomena brings may lead to the establishment of permanent relationships in which each belongs to the other. The avoidance of such ongoing partnerships must remain a matter of choice rather than an inability to become involved in such a way. When the prohibitions against fixed celebrative partnerships which come from the same sources as familial discipline are extended to all interpersonal interactions outside marriage, there is a loss of capacity for spontaneous self-expression and a limitation in the vigor which the personality can find.

Friendship between individuals of opposite character

establishes an interpersonal context in which the idealization of the masculinity of the one, and the constructive exploitation of the femininity of the other, lead to reinforcement of the inner identity as an end in itself. Such relationships have growth itself as their goal. This type of relationship is a unique product of civilization and, above all other psychological phenomena, is a potential source of the creative orientation and organization of the personality. This type of attachment and involvement between men brings an area of psychological life into being which is safe from the inroads of the social roles. It constitutes a human workshop where men can help each other find the ultimate in their opposite identities, and at the same time learn to face the unknown and the chaotic in the world around them. Because the demands of adaptive social living are kept outside the relationship, the reaching for self-realization through the search for human truth and right can proceed with continuity and integrity, preserving the adolescent spirit no matter how great the demands of adaptive maturity may be.

The mated structure of a relationship between opposites provides for a dependence in the finding of psychological balance and thereby releases the individual from much of his dependence on the support he would otherwise require from his social roles. His autonomous development is greatly facilitated by finding dependence on another person who is equally autonomous in his relationship to society. Since the relationship takes its being in surplus phenomena, it fulfills itself in expressing creative love and power on a personal basis between the partners. There can be no prohibition on sexual awareness and no refusal to accept the existence of celebrative drives. Under these circumstances, awareness of homosexual feeling on the part of the idealizing yielding individual, and acceptance of the assertive tendency to total possession of all surplus power assets, may become a part of the relationship. If these tendencies cannot be understood and handled in the partnership, the expanding nature of the relationship will be destroyed, and its capacity to reach creative meaning and value will be undermined. Unless such adolescent relationships bring the partners to a creative relationship to life itself, the relationship becomes a form of rebellion and heresy against maturity. If it is not creative in its implications, a deepening capacity for love becomes the basis of mental illness, and a widening scope of personal power becomes a form of running wild. Friendships which have a mated structure must find their own inner balance. It is the task of love to tame the potential wildness of surplus power; power undertakes to heal the potential sickness of surplus love.

THE MASCULINE COMMUNITY

Love which is its own end requires a context in which it has meaning in a world of experience. Without this context, it becomes a form of withdrawal which ultimately leads to a breakdown in the integrity of thought. Power which is its own end requires a context in which it has value in a world of responsive feeling. Without this context, it becomes isolated by indifference which leads to a deterioration of the capacity for continuity of involvement. Relationships between men of opposite character have special importance in the area of mental health and the control of antisocial tendencies. Men who live creative interpersonal lives have no guarantee that their personal insights and mastery will have a practical application to the adaptive goals of daily living. The truth and right bring their own rewards, because they constitute contributions to the ultimate welfare of society itself. The devotion of the self to the building of human wisdom and strength involves a risk of mental illness and social disharmony, and the individual who takes an independent course in the creative sphere must assume the responsibility of dealing on his own with these hazards.

When men join together for the mutual reinforcement of their creative identities they use each other for purposes which are essentially therapeutic in nature. In contrast to the mature adaptive goals where men are judged by their social accomplishments, the goals of a creative friendship are to be found in the development of the psychological tools for living, uninfluenced by considerations of conventional success. The establishment of a specialized character in a context where mental health and social harmony are preserved becomes the function of the masculine community. The putting aside of the conventional social roles is facilitated by this purely masculine environment in which women are admitted only on a limited basis. They may become elements in the identity seeking activities of men, or they may attain full fledged membership in those situations where they show themselves prepared to accept participation in the functions of the masculine community, in which case they become psychologically like men in their social separation from familial goals.

A special aspect of the masculine community is found in the monastic retreat, which provides for a permanent withdrawal from full scale involvement in the obligations of the masculine social role. The soldier's enlistment provides a similar outlet for those who require a total commitment based on separation from the social restraints associated with the conventional masculine identity. The service of truth under the protection of religious institutions provides a place for the depth within the personality without risking a personal struggle for identity in the market place of daily living. The adherence to the right under the encouragement of the military way of life provides an outlet for vigor within the personality without risking a personal struggle for identity in the commonplace circumstances of daily living.

When creative personalities seek and find an inner identity independently, making relationships within the masculine community without the guidance of established rules and authority, they must use insights and mastery which come to them as part of their social heritage. If the impact of adolescent growth carries them into the area of the un-known and the chaotic, their efforts at self-discovery will involve the additional task of bringing the psychological tools of growth into existence on their own. The struggle for an expanding self-knowledge and self-control will be short lived indeed if the individual is not prepared to live in such a way as to retain access to a long continuing search for truth and to an enduring exploration of the right. Such commitments prolong the adolescent spirit and interfere with any easy access to the social roles of adaptive maturity. The more the individual can resist the tendency to seek individuality through overinvestment in the patterns of maturity, the more access he can retain to the search for an individual identity. The search for individuality sets a process in motion which may not run its full course in an entire lifetime, and as each man lays down his task, others emerge to carry it forward. Thus is not only the adolescence of the individual prolonged, but in the evolution of the civilized way of life, the adolescence of the community be-comes an established aspect of social life, a fact which clearly emerges in periods of rapid social change.

Men use the masculine community as a means of retaining their selectivity and mobility under conditions which would otherwise be unfavorable for the expression of these psycho-logical capacities. The bringing into existence of an isolated aspect of the self which only emerges in a masculine environ-ment becomes necessary when the world of adaptive maturity shows itself resistant to the growth process and men must accept a fixed barrier between their growth tendencies and their adaptive life. The separate existence of a permanent adolescence confined to the special area of masculine comradeship provides the basis of a masculine community. If the growth processes break through the barrier, the superstructure of that part of maturity which is arbitrary and tyrannical may be swept away, and once this process is set in motion, there is no guarantee that change will stop at any safe point.

INHIBITION AND PERPLEXITY
IN MASCULINE RELATIONSHIPS

When men accept attachments and interests among each other for their own sake, they discover that higher levels of interaction are possible when masculine and feminine psychological tendencies reinforce each other. In this area of potentially creative interaction, each individual must find the way in which he is favorably influenced by the needs and purposes of other individuals. Only the trial and error of living human involvements can show him whether he can fulfill himself through any particular human attachment. The ultimate test of such relationships is provided by the evidence of personal development which comes from them. It is in the casting aside of useless fear and rage in an expanding world of warmth and pride that men know they are growing psychologically.

Within the masculine community, yielding personalities do not have easy access to mobility, since they reach masculine traits in a dependent fashion, and their masculinity is primarily attached to their mature social roles. Since this social masculinity becomes readily contaminated by aggression in the civilized world, it is in the masculine community that yielding personalities have the greatest opportunity to develop a masculine balance for the feminine core of the

self without becoming committed to aggressive mechanisms.
They attain this kind of development through a dependent
identification with a masculine ideal which is found outside
the circle of persons who are similar to themselves. When
the masculinity of yielding personalities can only come
through identification with the mature social masculinity
of the family, and especially the father or his psychological
representatives in the general community, the inner capacity
for idealization cannot find an adequate outlet and aggressive contamination of the personality becomes inevitable.

Within the masculine community, assertive personalities
cannot easily find selectivity, since they reach feminine
capacities in a dependent fashion, and their feminine traits
are primarily attached to their mature social roles. Since
this social feminine capacity is readily undermined by
passivity in the civilized world, it is in the masculine community that assertive personalities have the greatest opportunity to develop feminine balance for the masculine core
of the self without acceptance of passive mechanisms. They
attain this kind of development through a dependent empathy with the feminine capacities of another person, coming from outside the familial circle of similar personalities.
When the feminine capacities of assertive personalities can
only be found through empathy with mature family members, and especially through the acceptance of the social
conformity of the father and others like him, the inner
capacity for the exploitation of reality cannot find a free
outlet and resignation to passive surrender becomes inevitable.

The unstructured relationships of the masculine community favor selectivity and mobility. The yielding personality cannot find mobility without the help of others, and
if he cannot accept involvements which provide such help,
he finds himself in a state of inhibition and an accompanying sense of inferiority. Mobility which is used compulsively

to overcome the sense of inferiority brings anxiety. The fear of making idealizing relationships may leave the individual with a fixed inhibition which he can only relieve by a flight into a full involvement with his mature social identity. This alternative may reduce his inhibitions and cure his anxiety, but only to the degree that he accepts an exclusion from the unstructured interactions of the masculine community. The arbitrary quality of the maturity he finds brings him into the shadow of potential depression. Genuine psychological growth is beyond his reach, and he fights against loss of enthusiasm by the overinvestment of the self in the self-aggrandizing aspects of his mature life.

The assertive personality cannot find selectivity except under the influence of others, and if he cannot make the attachments from which such influences flow, he finds himself in a state of perplexity and an associated sense of guilt. Superficial attachments which are used obsessively to overcome guilt bring pathological restlessness. The tendency to experience diffuse rage in the absence of an established sense of belonging with others undermines the individual's confidence in his self-control and may leave him unable to shift into new areas of genuine attachments. This paralysis of selectivity brings a fixed perplexity which he can only relieve by a full espousal of the patterns of conformity of his mature social identity. This alternative may reduce his perplexity and overcome his restlessness but only on the conditions that he make a permanent renunciation of free interactions in the masculine community. The tyrannical quality of the maturity he finds brings him into a barren land where depression becomes inevitable. He can only deal with this threat to his capacity for inspiration by an overinvestment of his psychological energies in mature channels, seeking gratification of his vanity as a substitute for growth.

Without an idealizing love which exists for its own sake, the yielding individual cannot become involved in a depend-

ent relationship to power which is its own end. Without a
capacity for power which is free to exploit any opportunity
for its own sake, the assertive individual cannot make a
place for dependence on love attachments which are ends
in themselves. The meaning and value of interpersonal relationships in the masculine community are to be found
in the surplus interactions between love and power. Love
can accept an unlimited access to its own depth of feeling
in a context brought into being by power. In any other context love feeds on itself and unrestricted love feeling becomes a form of illness in which love must ultimately idealize
itself. Power can accept an unlimited access to its own
capacity for the expression of vigorous attitudes in a context
created by love. In any other context power competes with
itself, and an unconfined power drive becomes antisocial
in nature, being guided only by the need to outdo what
it has done before. This kind of self-development is not
anchored in constructiveness and leads the power strivings
of man into channels where the elaboration of Gargantuan
capacities undermines productivity.

When love finds the security which power creates, there
is a harmonious acceptance of any depth of feeling, and in
such a psychological context sexual feeling emerges whenever the tasks of love no longer require a full commitment
of psychic energies. The sexual component of idealizing love
cannot be permitted to replace its devotion to the truth
seeking process, but when the work of creative thought
reaches the endpoint of insight, there is a release from effort
which makes room for sexualization of feeling. If this sexuality is alien to the personality and dangerous to the image of
the self, there can be no successful working through of the
need for idealized relationships. It is the tendency of such
feeling to be expressed homosexually which causes men
to turn away from experiential involvement in a genuine
power world.

When power finds the freedom which love makes possible, there is a spontaneous acceptance of any level of vigor of the self, and in such a psychological context celebration enters whenever the search for involvement no longer requires a full measure of psychic tension. The celebrative component of constructive power cannot be allowed to replace its responsibility for the reaching for the right, but when the experimental explorations come to an end through the emergence of mastery, there is a release from tension bearing which makes room for a celebrative overflow. If this channel of celebrative expression is alien to the personality and dangerous to the social balance of the individual, there can be no successful working through of the need for exploitative relationships with other men. It is the tendency of such attitudes to be expressed in the formation of relatively fixed masculine partnerships which causes men to turn away from the sources of love among each other.

CREATIVITY IN MASCULINE RELATIONSHIPS

In the world of adaptive maturity, masculinity and femininity are identified through their obvious surface traits, based in part on biological gender differences, but primarily on elaboration of the social roles. Masculine and feminine identity of this kind is relatively fixed, not being subject to alteration in the personal development of the individual. Like any other aspect of the mature adaptive social life, these roles are taken to be unchanging and inevitable, and any deviation is received as a form of rebellion or heresy. Changes come in this area only through the growth of society itself. When significant changes in masculine and feminine social identity do come, it is always an indication of major social instability.

Within the masculine community there are psychological contexts of a creative nature which are above and beyond the direct influence and control of socially established masculinity and femininity. Men have masculine and feminine interpersonal involvements with each other, based on an inner search for meaning and value for their own sake, without regard for fixed social images and forms. Such interactions are not usually seen or handled as expressions of masculinity and femininity because such a classification comes into conflict with the generally accepted criteria of gender differences, but when the search for an inner identity reaches the point where sexual and celebrative components emerge in relationships between men, awareness of a feminine or masculine identity in that context becomes inevitable. Such development remains a psychological matter in which the individual discovers tendencies originating within himself and does not consist of accepting a role imposed from without.

Men need to be able to identify deep submissive tendencies as feminine and vigorous dominant tendencies as masculine because they lead into surplus manifestations which they must handle in an autonomous way. Society seeks to confine these phenomena by attaching them exclusively to the relationships between men and women. When idealizing love awakens sexuality of a homosexual nature, the individual must have the psychological resources for maintaining the unity of his personality. If he chooses to recognize the homosexual tendency within himself, he develops a self-image which includes a feminine inner identity. Such femininity is purely psychological and has its own private existence as far as the social roles are concerned. The individual is able to recognize a meaningful feminine identity within himself which in no way interferes with the expression of the masculine social role in other appropriate contexts. Entirely without regard to whether the individual enters a homosexual relationship or not, it is absolutely essential to the development of a creative interpersonal life for him to be capable of accepting an inner identity which comes from his own autonomous search for love and which is not guided or distorted by his social need to perform in an established masculine pattern. Without this kind of psychological independence, the search for inner security and the creative productivity it brings must fail.

When exploitative power arouses the need for possessive attachments between men, the dominant individual must have the psychological resources for maintaining the continuity of his inner identity. If he accepts his possessive tendencies at a celebrative level, he must develop a personal masculine identity which has its own existence and is of a separate nature as far as the social roles are concerned. Whether he becomes involved in possessive attachments with others of his own sex or not, the ability to deal with these tendencies is an irreducible necessity for the development of a creative interpersonal life. He must be able to find an inner identity through his autonomous reaching for personal power, unalloyed with the established forms of mature masculine performance. Without this kind of psychological independence, the search for inner freedom and its associated productivity must fail.

It is only when love and power come together in a union which has mutual self-development as its goal that men can fulfill all their inner potential for specialized character development. If society is to have access to the accumulation of new truth and right which is the basis of social progress, creative individuals must lead personal lives which make a place for the expansion of inner security and freedom, and this place must have an independent existence which neither interferes with their mature adaptation nor accepts interference from it. There can be no ultimate security without a sense of permanence, and there can be no genuine freedom without a context which brings an uncompromising integrity into being. The union of love and power for its own sake creates this psychological atmosphere. Permanence implies a complete self-exposure in which honesty has no barriers in its path. There must be some part of life in which the individual has nothing to gain from ignorance of any element of what he feels, no matter how far he may go in exposing his inner nature. Integrity implies an inner readiness for continuity of involvement in which courage accepts no fragmentation of its expression. There must be some part of life in which the individual has nothing to gain by avoidance of any element of his potential for self-expression, no matter how far he may go in the mobilization of his capacity for molding his human environment.

THE MATED UNION IN
MASCULINE RELATIONSHIPS

If love is to do its creative work in the world without vulnerability to promiscuous sexualization on the one hand, or to loss of capacity for unlimited access to feeling on the other, the yielding personality must be able to reach understanding of the psychological roots of sexuality under circumstances which permit a full range of exploration, trial and error, and harmonious self-acceptance. No individual can really know himself without a genuine comprehension of his sexual potential in any context which the circumstances of a selective and mobile interpersonal creativity bring into being. Hidden sexual tendencies never remain completely hidden from the self but tend to emerge in the form of fantasy which is fragmented from the image of the self as a whole and has a strong potential for accumulating shame. When sexual fantasy brings a sense of inferiority, inhibition limits the capacity to enter experience. The individual must avoid those interpersonal situations where sexual responsiveness tends to emerge, and since there is an inherent attraction to such situations, his growth struggles are either dominated by anxiety or abandoned entirely.

If personal power is to find a world of creative interpersonal opportunity without falling prey to indiscriminate celebration on the one hand, or to loss of capacity for unlimited participation in experience on the other, the assertive personality must have access to control of the celebrative impulses wherever circumstances bring them into being, and the individual cannot do this without a self-confident acceptance of himself in experimental situations. No individual has really attained self-control until he has been exposed to the full impact of the celebrative drives which are released in the selective and mobile world brought into being by creative interpersonal relationships. Dissociated celebrative tendencies never remain completely alien to the sense of personal identity, but tend to enter the personality through transient episodes of play-acting and these moments of willful behavior have a strong potential for accumulating guilt. When celebrative play-acting is eliminated by avoiding the attachments which release it, perplexity limits the capacity for cohesive feeling. The individual must resist the temptation to participate in those situations where celebrative expressiveness tends to emerge, and since he is drawn to such situations, his growth struggles are either dominated by restlessness or given up entirely.

It is in the nature of sexual pleasure that it seeks to fulfill itself in a context where no aspect of desire must be denied, and celebrative enjoyment reaches toward those interpersonal contexts where no aspect of eager purposefulness must be refused expression. The mated context established in nature by the union of male and female meets these requirements. No matter how much men elaborate and reinforce the sexual and celebrative components of familial relationships, they cannot go beyond the fact that social custom and convention are guiding and controlling their feelings and attitudes. If they become heretical and rebellious in this psychological area, they not only undermine the continuity and integrity of social ideas and institutions, but the misuse of familial interpersonal relationships exposes them to the impossible task of keeping growth forces alive in circumstances which are inherently unfavorable.

It is in the masculine community that men find a psychological atmosphere in which inner growth can proceed without limit and at the same time offer no inevitable threat to the stability of basic social standards of maturity. The more growth strivings are given room for expression in the masculine community, the more the psychologically masculine and the psychologically feminine in that community seek involvement with each other. This context is entirely favorable to the gratification of any longing and to the accomplishment of any vigilant purpose. Where the context reaches a mated structure, there is no inherent barrier to the sexual and celebrative overflow which characterizes the mated union in nature. Under such circumstances men must learn to take cognizance of their homosexual feelings and possessive attitudes toward each other. The only way that such relationships can survive in the presence of these tendencies is for men to take independent responsibility for what they feel and do, working through their emerging self-awareness and self-confidence without regard for the prohibitions and restraints imposed from without.

In a world where homosexual feeling is feared as a threat to the masculine social role, the yielding personality must find a channel for the development of the love capacities which permits the individual full access to his idealization of masculinity without encroaching on the areas which belong to his socially established masculinity. If he cannot muster the resources for this psychologically complex and difficult autonomous undertaking, his homosexual tendencies will bring an increasing burden of anxiety whenever inner growth processes are at work. When the fear of homosexuality is accepted as an inevitable component of psychological maturity, becoming part of the image of normalcy for the whole community, the love which men bear for each other must fail to reach that depth and continuity which are required for the creative solution of human problems. This state of affairs not only undermines the mental health of individuals but brings the survival of civilization itself into question.

In a world where masculine celebrative partnerships are not acceptable as a harmonious part of psychological experience, the emergence of such attachments threatens to bring rage reactions into focus within the personality. The assertive personality in a state of growth must find channels which permit the individual full access to his need for exploitation of human resources without encroaching on the areas which belong to the established patterns of his social masculine role. His free masculine inner identity is untrammeled in structure; his social masculine role is not. If he cannot muster the resources for the complex and difficult search for a psychologically independent masculinity, his tendency for involvement in masculine partnerships will bring an increasing burden of restlessness whenever growth processes are stimulated. If the necessity to avoid masculine attachments for their own sake is accepted as an inevitable requirement of psychological maturity, becoming part of the image of normalcy for the whole community, the personal power which men seek to share together must fail to reach that vigor and integrity which are required for the creative dealing with human frustrations and obstacles. Under these conditions, men are vulnerable to antisocial deterioration of their gregarious loyalties, and their capacity to take responsibility for the survival of civilization itself is compromised.

Homosexual feeling is less threatening to the conventional masculine role when it is excluded from experience within the masculine community. If it remains afloat within the personality without a base from which its origins, meaning, and consequences may be perceived and understood, it threatens to emerge in an irrational and disorderly way, rendering its encroachment on maturity patterns more likely. This kind of shadow manipulation of homosexuality, in which it is confined within the area of the unknown, creates superficiality which men really have to fear because it renders cynical and unimportant the search for self-knowledge in human relationships.

Masculine partnerships are less threatening to the conventional masculine role when they are excluded from reaching an on-going status within the masculine community. If they remain a matter of episodic gregariousness, without a base from which their total implications and value can be developed and brought within the scope of personal responsibility, they press for emergence in an immoral and disorganized way, rendering encroachment on maturity patterns more likely. This lack of integrity in dealing with the free celebrative tendencies, in which they are assigned to the domain of the chaotic, creates weakness which really threatens the stability of social institutions, because it brings opportunism into the search for self-mastery in human relationships.

The exclusion of homosexual feeling from access to experience and the isolation of celebrative partnerships from access to lasting attachments are reinforced within the masculine community by the maintenance of a social barrier between its yielding and assertive elements. As long as yielding personalities idealize a false aggressive masculinity which comes from themselves, they can dwell behind this protecting wall with some sense of inner security, provided that they are not exposed to the need for inner growth. As long as assertive personalities exploit a human reality which comes out of the passive feminine components in themselves, they can operate within their permissive world with some sense of inner freedom, provided they are not committed to a need for personal growth. Those individuals who break through the barrier and make common cause with men different from themselves must pass through a development which no longer concedes the unknown status of homosexuality nor the chaotic nature of celebrative partnerships. Such men can make the inroads on human ignorance and immorality which the survival of civilization requires.

PERVERSION AND ADDICTION IN THE MASCULINE COMMUNITY

When the masculine community functions to create human contexts where all that is unknown and chaotic within the personality can be brought within the scope of faith and hope, the functional difference between growth phenomena and the life of adaptive maturity is brought into focus. The key to this division lies in the privacy and separateness of the autonomous interpersonal involvements of growth and the contrasting exposure of the self to the need for social acceptance and recognition in the area of maturity. Maturity has no meaning or value unless it is successful in its own terms. Maturity is judged by the continuity and effectiveness of its conformity to the immediate adaptive needs of society. The obligations and duties of maturity cannot be allowed to expand for their own sake; when they do, they become arbitrary and tyrannical. Creative maturity does not consist of an intimate mingling of the creative and the mature aspects of psychological life but of a stable separation between them in which creativity pursues its own independent ends under the protection of privacy and separateness, and maturity serves the established goals provided by social ideas and institutions.

One of the great psychological tasks of maturity is the acceptance of sex and celebration under the conditions of control imposed by the family structure of society. Any other outlets of sex and celebration must be evaluated and judged by the individual in terms of their overall psychological effect on his mental health and capacity for social harmony. The mature outlets for sex and celebration are not discovered by the individual and are not subject to the changes brought by the personal search for human understanding and responsibility. The individual attains a good adjustment in the sexual and celebrative sphere when these forces have been channeled into patterns which are generally accepted without question. Any deviation from this path constitutes a provocation to society which exposes the individual to the loss of the automatic social acceptance which maturity brings. Because the place of the surpluses in a mature world is not subject to individual question, changes can only come as social ideas and institutions change through the operation of social progress. Man has much to learn about the sources and nature of his sexual feelings, and has a long way to go in developing a reliable control of all aspects of his celebrative attitudes. New knowledge of sexuality and new ability in dealing with celebration cannot be allowed to overwhelm the stability of the mature familial outlets.

Truth and right in human affairs have no necessary or inevitable relationship to the life of maturity at any given time and place in the civilized world. As long as truth and right guide the growth processes of men, they will fulfill their destiny in shaping social progress, and it is in the world of tomorrow, never today, that the ultimate hegemony of truth and right is to be found. This means that new insights and mastery are not necessarily welcome in the world of maturity, and this is nowhere more obvious than in the sexual and celebrative sphere. As men become more aware of their sexuality, and more capable of using all aspects of their celebrative drives, they tend to come into conflict with the mature standards in these areas. They become increasingly able to identify perverse or addicted mechanisms as such, whether they are generally recognized to be so or not. The way these phenomena are seen does not have to alter the social image of what is normal, at least until society is ready to allow the alteration to come, but the social image of normalcy cannot be allowed to destroy man's capacity for independent insight and mastery in human affairs. Men must have an area in life where they think and act for themselves in the pursuit of insight and mastery for their own sake, without regard to the social standards of normalcy. Without access to this creative form of interpersonal life, the science of human nature cannot grow nor can the development of new modalities of human control proceed forward.

Men accept perversity and addiction when these mechanisms serve the interests of a mature social adjustment. When perversity and addiction enter the area of the creative search for inner identity, they undermine the capacity of love to reach the service of an ideal, and of power to find the constructive exploitation of opportunity. Perverse mechanisms become readily recognizable as such when they are no longer camouflaged by social acceptance, and addiction provokes social opposition when it overflows the channels of the socially permissible. When homosexuality becomes the basis of a deviant kind of family life, forming the basis of a homosexual community in the process, it develops its own kind of social roles and its own standards of maturity. The surface feminine traits of individuals who accept a feminine role in a homosexual community are characterized by an artificial effeteness, losing access to the creative capacities which bring love into relationship with the world of universal experience. Masculine elements in such a community are often not truly assertive in their basic character, but express a contrived and pretentious masculine posture.

When masculine celebrative partnerships become the basis of a deviant kind of substitute for family life in which the sharing of interests creates a stable bond between men in gregarious patterns, they live a mobile life characterized by membership in a community of vagabonds. The fraternity of individuals on the move in life develops its own kind of social roles and its own standards of maturity. Masculine traits in such a community are exaggerated in a pattern of insensitivity to personal needs, leading to a brutalization of the self and a loss of access to the creative capacities and to the loyalties which genuine power brings. Feminine psychological elements in such a community are not usually the product of a true yielding in the character, but arise from a parasitic helplessness which reinforces the pride of others for its own opportunistic purposes.

The homosexual community falls prey to the same perverse self-serving tendencies which its members find so objectionable in society as a whole, but they do avoid the aggressive corruption of the personality which would otherwise overwhelm them. Because of the withdrawal inherent in membership in such a community, paranoid degeneration of the patterns of thought is common, and addiction mechanisms, if they do emerge, are extremely dangerous to the equilibrium of the personality. The fraternal community of unattached individuals is vulnerable to the same addiction to pretentious vanity which its members reject when it is expressed in conventional ways, but they do avoid the passive temptations which would otherwise overcome them. Because of the indifference inherent in their relationship to the whole of society, criminal deterioration of the patterns of action is common, and perverse mechanisms, if they do emerge, become extremely dangerous to the equilibrium of the personality.

It can be said that the homosexual community is formed on the basis that those who participate in it have lost faith in the integrity of power in the world. Its members refuse to worship the aggressive usurpers of the masculine function in the whole of society. The homosexual community, like the institution of religion itself, constitutes a reservoir of love in the world which is capable of preserving itself in otherwise unfavorable circumstances, and although it cannot do the creative work of love out of its own psychological resources, it stands as an indestructible reminder that the love of which men are capable has not yet found a home on earth that is worthy of its potentialities.

The community of men who have the vagabond spirit is formed on the basis of a loss of hope for the kind of opportunity which love can offer. Its members refuse to become involved in the passive distortions of the feminine principle as expressed in society in general. The fraternal community of unattached persons, like military organization itself, constitutes a reservoir of personal power in the world which exists above and beyond circumstance, and although it cannot find a world for creative constructive action, it carries the banner of a personal refusal to compromise high in the air for all to see so that men must ultimately recognize that all the power which men can mobilize has not yet found a home on earth that is worthy of its capabilities.

PART III

INDIVIDUAL GROWTH
AND SOCIAL PROGRESS

CREATIVITY AND SOCIAL STABILITY

The utilization of love and power in a mature world follows the channels established by family ties and career involvements. Because of the tendency to invest a great deal of the psychic tensions and energies in the undertakings of maturity, the preservation of the areas which belong to the creative spirit becomes difficult or impossible for many people. The channeling of all of the self into mature activities confers the immediate advantage of providing love with direct gratifications in which faith has no major tasks, and it provides power a field of operation in which hope does not have to take the risks of an experimental world. When needs and goals are clearly established in socially reinforced patterns, the individual utilizes patience and endurance only insofar as learning and asset accumulation are tools for his adaptive purposes. The love he invests is valid from the beginning and it accepts problems only to the degree that it must in order to survive in a world where hate is also a psychological necessity. Such love cannot seek out problems for their own sake, and it shuns the unknown wherever possible. Personal power is keyed to established types of opportunity and it deals with obstacles only to the degree that it must in order to remain effective in an anger provoking world. Such power cannot explore obstacles as an end in itself, and it avoids the chaotic whenever possible.

A further immediate advantage comes to individuals who have no reservations in their espousal of maturity through the use of warmth and pride as a direct means of building adaptive relationships. The cultivation of personal warmth for its adaptive effectiveness tends to ignore honesty. Love which comes out of interpersonal relationships in which honesty is not important cannot find the balance which is characteristic of the interaction between truth and right. Artificially cultivated love is only valid when it obtains its intended response. It cannot find new understanding out of itself, and therefore seeks to perpetuate itself by the manipulation of others. In such manipulative activity, standards of morality are swept away by the emergency nature of the inner needs. That which began in love ends in aggression. There is an especial brutality in aggression because it comes to its task armed with the analytic tools which love has brought into being.

The cultivation of personal pride for the sake of its usefulness in adaptive relationships tends to flourish without regard for the scope and continuity which come from the influence of courage. Power which develops where courage is not important tends to be an unbalanced phenomenon. Such power is only recognizable through the prestige it accumulates. It cannot find new capacities for responsibility out of itself, and therefore seeks to maintain its hegemony through the invoking of the personal adoration of others. As it reaches out to attract love, illusion replaces genuine awareness, and anything which triggers responsive feeling becomes acceptable due to the emergency nature of the inner drives. That which began in the functions of power loses its way in the enchantments of passivity. There is an especial sentimentality in passivity because it is fascinated by the attachments which the inventiveness of power has brought into being.

Love which channels itself in familial attachments and their derivatives in the community readily finds balance through the sense of duty. It is in the expanding adherence to duty that the individual expresses the goodness that orients love in such a way as to be free of inhibitions. It is on the pathway of goodness that yielding personalities are able to elaborate the masculine social role which is the carrier of their social identity. Power which expresses itself through family attachments and their derivates in the community finds balance readily through the loyalties thus generated. It is through the associated inner completeness that the individual finds the pride in his own integrity which organizes power in such a way as to be free of perplexity. An expanding integrity embodies beauty, and under its influence assertive personalities are able to elaborate the feminine components of their social role which are essential to its social identity.

Goodness which is tied to family interests can only expand as family needs grow greater, and the dutiful person finds himself immeshed in a reaching for power as a means of satisfying needs which have no necessary limit. The psychological structure of this kind of power seeking is compulsive and lacks creative implications. An autocratic taskmaster takes residence within the self, and although the individual is altruistic in relationship to the needs of those he loves, he sees these family members as extensions of himself, and ultimately the autocracy is expressed toward them. His family altruism puts the stamp of goodness on his life, and his awareness of immorality in his relationships with outsiders shrinks to the point where independent self-evaluation is lost. As long as he remains within the boundaries established by law, he finds himself to be moral. This rigidity of moral standards leads to a state of affairs in which immoral social influences come from the lives of good men.

Beauty which takes its being exclusively in the atmosphere

of family attachments can only expand as the undertakings of the family extend into new areas, and the individual finds himself unendingly involved in love commitments which are used to gain access to more channels of pride-serving activity. The psychological structure of this kind of love seeking is obsessive and is without creative implications. A dogmatic lawgiving function dominates the inner self, and although the individual plays a heroic role in the family constellation, he deals with family members as extensions of himself and requires of them a similar arbitrary loyalty. His familial heroic role creates the aura of beauty in his life, and he can reject any necessity to become aware of the degenerate implications of his own superficiality through ignoring the influence of outsiders. As long as he maintains the necessary minimal social cooperation, the sources of his sense of pride need not be subject to analysis. This rigidity in the capacity to evaluate his own kind leads to a state of affairs in which the degenerate influence of social ignorance is reinforced by the lives of men who embody high standards of personal honor.

CONTENTMENT AND HAPPINESS

When love expends itself primarily in the performance of mature duties, the individual expects to be rewarded for his goodness by peace of mind and a sense of security in his relationship with society, but inner security can attain continuity only through a readiness to give love for its own sake. Material security, on the other hand, is sought as a means of providing for the needs of the self and those who are extensions of the self, and this type of security must be measured against expanding needs which do not have any established limit. Yesterday's sense of security may be quite inadequate in the circumstances of tomorrow. When discontent threatens the personality on a depressive basis, the individual seeks new needs so that he may rediscover the security which comes when he succeeds in gratifying new desires. The multiplication of needs becomes an anti-depressive mechanism and involves the individual in a search for power assets which cannot come to rest. Such power strivings are self-aggrandizing in the extreme.

When power fulfills itself primarily in mature responsibil-ities, the individual expects to be rewarded for his honorable behavior by a sense of release from further involvements and a resulting mood of freedom in his relationship with society, but inner freedom depends on the sense of his own expansive integrity, which rests on making power its own goal. Freedom which depends on social acceptance is of a different kind. It seeks recognition for the self and those who are extensions of the self, and this kind of freedom can only bring inner happiness when popularity provides an expanding world of social opportunity. The social interests of yesterday may become the confinements of tomorrow. When unhappiness threatens the personality on a depressive basis, the individual seeks new goals so that he may redis-cover the freedom which comes out of his new accomplish-ments. The multiplication of goals becomes an antidepres-sive mechanism and involves the individual in a reaching for the love responses of others which can never fully find satisfaction. Such love strivings originate in an extreme form of vanity.

The immorality of good men invades their way of life out of a betrayal wrought by their altruistic devotion to the welfare of their own kind. Within the circle of family life and its immediate extensions in the community, they elabo-rate all the empathetic mechanisms of love. This emersion in the giving and receiving of the rewards of love is a means of holding depressive aspects of their maturity at bay. The power component of life is taken for granted. This auto-matic acceptance of power drives which are not subject to the influence of the highest standards of creative interpersonal behavior, being outside the realm of growth which autonomous personal power brings into being, results in the espousal of a kind of power which is readily captured by emergency reactions. Such power does not build a better home on earth for all men, but aggrandizes the self and the loved ones who belong to the self. Although such men live in the name of love, their social morality is not the product of it, and the only ultimate control over their power strivings is to be found in the enforceable laws of society itself.

The spiritual lack of depth which maturity imposes on men of strength in the civilized world is the price they pay for their access to leadership of their own kind. Within the circle of family life and its extensions in the community, they devote themselves to an elaboration of pride and honor. They walk in the ways of power, giving and receiving its rewards as a means of keeping depressive aspects of maturity at bay. The love component of life is taken for granted. This dogmatic adherence to channels of love feeling which are not subject to the influence of the highest capacities for creative awareness, being outside the realm of growth which autonomous love brings, results in the acceptance of the kind of love which is readily invaded by emergency reactions. Such love does not lead to deepening understanding among all men, but serves the egotism of the self and those who belong to the self. Although such men embody power in their lives, their social philosophy is not a responsible part of it, and their social empathy accepts no alien elements except when tolerance is enforced by established social conventions.

Men long for peace of mind and the contentment which goes with it. If they attempt to buy this state of inner security through the accumulation of material assets, they find themselves on a treadmill which disrupts the inner identity on which psychological security depends. If they are not to sell their souls in the process of seeking a successful mature adjustment, they must bring an inner identity to living which has been firmly established in an adolescent growth period. This identity can only find meaning through the access it gives to growth itself. Permanency can only come to the love capacities when they exist as an independent aspect of the self, above and beyond any immediate reward love can attain. Without faith in the capacity of human integrity to embody beauty, love must fail to supply the key to the growth of the personality.

Men search eagerly for a spontaneous involvement in life and the mood of happiness which goes with it. If they attempt to win this state of inner freedom through the cultivation of automatic social acceptance, their ability to charm others becomes the measure of value in interpersonal relationships. This emphasis on personal attractiveness disrupts the inner identity on which psychological freedom depends. If men are not to lose their souls in the reaching for a successful mature adaptation, they must bring a pre-existing integrity to living which has been formed in an adolescent growth process. This identity gains its value from the access it gives to growth itself. Completeness within itself can only come to the power capacities when they have an independent existence above and beyond any immediate rewards which power can attain. Without hope which is based on the continuity of responsiveness of human goodness, power must fail to establish itself as the key to the growth capacities.

THE RETREAT AND THE ENLISTMENT

The easy path to maturity for yielding personalities lies through a cynical rejection of love in dealing with the competitive struggles of the adaptive life. Men reach this view of life because they find love at odds with the goals of their power strivings. Love cannot survive in contexts where men believe in power which is not creative in its implications. If love becomes attached to that which is inherently unlovable, the individual can only become mentally ill. Where men give up love in favor of a fascination with a false aggressive ideal, there is actually no psychological loss for the individual at the adaptive level. Society is the loser, and the individual only pays the price as the later manifestations of a defective inner identity emerge. The cause of this failure of love does not lie in the competitive nature of maturity itself, but in the inability of love to come to the tasks of maturity with an already established creative love capacity.

Assertive personalities find easy access to maturity through an opportunistic rejection of responsibility in the course of their struggle for recognition in the adaptive world. Men reach this way of life because they find personal power in conflict with their need for automatic acceptance. Power cannot survive in contexts where it exploits love which is not creative in its implications. If power attempts to possess that which is inherently hostile to exploitation, the individual can only become antisocial. When men abandon personal power in favor of the enchantments of a false passive reality, there is no psychological loss for the individual at the adaptive level, but his future growth capacities are compromised, and his influence on expanding social responsibility ceases to exist. The cause of this failure of power does not lie in the seductive influences of maturity, but in the inability of personal power to come to the involvements of maturity with an already established power capacity.

It may be said that social progress hinges on the bringing of the accomplishments of love and power into the daily affairs of human beings. Love which is corrupted by the taking of the aggressive route to maturity cannot find an ideal worthy of itself. If love is to preserve its truth finding function, it must be prepared to withdraw whenever the circumstances of mature adaptation make its corruption inevitable. The monastic retreat becomes the means by which men maintain the continuity of love in its universal and permanent aspects. From the reservoir of creative love which is preserved by religion, men make attempts to carry its sensitivity into a world of experience where autonomous creativity can flourish. This undertaking proceeds slowly because the applications of love have revolutionary implications which are resisted in the name of the stability of social institutions, and because the emergence of love from protected surroundings results in an exposure to corrupting forces which tends to destroy its creative identity.

Power which is weakened by the taking of the passive route to maturity cannot find a world of opportunity which is worthy of itself. If power is to preserve its function of establishing the right, it must be prepared to become indifferent to involvements whenever the undermining of its capacity for personal responsibility becomes the inevitable price of maturity. The military type of enlistment creates a reservoir of personal power which men attempt to apply in their freely chosen creative relationships. This undertaking is very difficult because power has heretical implications which tend to weaken the reliability of social beliefs, and because power tends to lose its creative identity when it leaves the military *esprit de corps* behind to expose itself to the temptations of an undisciplined world.

Men can only bring an increasing investment of love into their lives of mature adaptation through the gradual evolution of social ideas and institutions which comes from social progress. If the personal love capacities of the individual are invested where there is no place for them, the practical goals of adaptation are compromised. Since the individual has more depth than he can use adaptively, the tendencies which belong to his creative nature must find appropriate ways to reach expression. The primary outlet for creative love in interpersonal relationships is the search for truth in human affairs. When the individual is forced into a retreat in order to preserve the love orientation of the inner self, his access to personal growth will be reduced insofar as the retreat creates a barrier to new experience. To overcome this isolation, the religious retreat may become a base for doing good deeds in the world, turning toward those elements in society which are socially deprived. This kind of love is parental in quality and avoids both revolutionary implications and the corrupting influences of full scale social participation. The disadvantage of this kind of service to society is that the growth of the individual becomes artificially limited, and the search for truth ceases to expand. Man cannot reduce the amount of hatred in the world by avoiding those situations where hatred would be aroused. If love needs helplessness in others for its expression, it is false in nature and must collapse in the face of a full scale impact with the living realities of ugly and destructive phenomena. It is only when men maintain a relationship with all aspects of the human world, living within the framework of their own time and place, that the creative work of love can win battles against the unknown in human nature.

Men bring personal power into their life of mature adaptation to the degree that stable social ideas and institutions provide opportunity. If the power organization of the individual seeks expression where it does not belong, the practical goals of adaptation are compromised. Since the individual has more vigor than he can use adaptively, he must find appropriate outlets in the creative interpersonal sphere. The primary outlet for creative personal power consists in the establishing of the self as an embodiment of the right in human affairs. When the individual must utilize indifference in order to preserve the power organization of the inner self, his access to growth will be com-

promised insofar as he is unable to develop new loyalties.
To overcome this detachment, the enlistment in heroic
and adventuresome undertakings may become the means
for developing lasting involvements. This kind of power
compels the adoration of those who follow its leadership.
It establishes a special domain for daring and courageous
action which avoids both heretical implications and the
exposure to temptations inherent in adaptive conformity.
The disadvantage of this kind of embodiment of the masculine ideal is that it is attached to unique conditions, and
the reaching for the right in the whole range of human
affairs ceases to grow from within the self. Man cannot
reduce the amount of anger in the world by ignoring those
human contexts where anger would be aroused. The power
posture created by the seeking of danger in order to attract
the admiration of others is actually superficial in nature
and is deflated when it encounters the challenge of immoral
phenomena. It is only when men accept involvement with
all the aspects of their human world, participating fully in
the events of their own time and place, that they can use
their creative power capacities to overcome the chaotic in
their relationships with each other.

PHILOSOPHY AND ART

The search for truth for its own sake cannot survive when
thinking becomes compulsive in nature. Creative thought
must remain free to respect the unity of its subject matter.
The thinker cannot become willful in the manipulation of
his conceptual awareness of the world because if he allows
himself to choose what aspect of the whole he will accept
as worthy of the search for knowledge, this aspect usurps
the place of the whole and expanding awareness ends. The
creative thinker must be able to come into relationship
with the totality of human experience in such a way that

there is no established limit on his psychological access to
new experience. He cannot find the communicability inherent in the truth without the universality of insight which
unlimited exposure to human psychological phenomena
brings. If he perverts his creative capacities for adaptive
goals, limits are automatically set to the scope of his awareness of human nature. Love is blind only in the sense that
the stable and mature love relationships must be taken
for granted as part of their stability. Creative love is never
blind. Thinking becomes compulsive when the need for an
expanding inner awareness comes up against a stable and
fixed world of experience where the individual's inner
withdrawal renders mobility impossible.

Men cannot embody right in their personal lives as an
end in itself when their access to modes of behavior is
limited by obsessive mechanisms. Creative action must be
free to develop the permanent aspect of the resources it
utilizes. If the man of action becomes self-conscious in his
inventive exploration of the world, he is unable to detect
those new aspects of flexibility and responsiveness which
lead on to the finding of lasting techniques of mastery, un-
contaminated by subjectivity. If he accepts mastery in the
moment, ignoring the fact that special circumstances produce
opportunity that is unique and will not recur, he will not
reach the permanence on which the demonstrable right
depends for its objectivity. The creative builder in human
affairs must be able to come into relationship with human
nature in such a way that there is no limit on his psychological access to all the potentialities of responsive feeling. If
he distorts his creative capacities for adaptive purposes, he
limits the scope of his self-confidence in dealing with others.
Power is never impotent in the presence of opportunity
except in the sphere of stable and mature power relationships where the channels of involvement are taken for
granted as part of their stability. Creative power never fails

to take advantage of any genuine human opportunity. The scope of action is limited by obsessive mechanisms when the need for an expanding inner self-confidence comes up against a stable and fixed world of human feeling, and the individual cannot enlarge his attachments because his inner indifference renders selectivity impossible.

The thinker is an observer of life who must live in such a way that his vantage point of observation can meet the requirements of truth seeking, providing him with the scope of vision suited to the questions being asked. In a monastic retreat the contemplation of truth takes revealed truth as its subject matter. The task of the monastic personality is to perfect its submission to life through the awareness of a particular kind of generalized truth, abandoning worldly self-aggrandizement in the process. The individual becomes a carrier of the creative love function, but does not necessarily make a personal contribution to the winning of territory from the unknown. The inner psychological security which comes from the contemplative religious life creates a need for intellectual labor which becomes channeled into philosophical preoccupations. Philosophy cannot flourish merely on the basis of the communication of concepts between philosophers, but must find an involvement with experience which is worthy of the submissive potential of the thinker, leading on to an idealization of the external world which is sufficient to produce meaningful insights. There is no value in asking questions unless men are in the position to search for answers. Neither can men profit from a potential for analytic thinking unless they are capable of asking questions which are of sufficient importance to justify the commitment they are prepared to make.

The man of action is participant in the concrete immediacy of the moment, guiding his activities into the channels of the right through awareness of the actual resources of the environment. His access to opportunity must be suited to the scope of his energy investment, requiring the undertaking of the kind of challenging projects which match his psychological stature and posture. Strength and courage emerge in relationship to the circumstances which require their employment. The enlistment in great undertakings of a military type endows the individual with an *esprit de corps* which spares him from a personal search for worthy purposes. Within the context of involvement in such undertakings, the individual can perfect his dominance of circumstance, avoiding the petty vanities of worldly living in the process. He becomes a carrier of the creative power function but does not necessarily make a personal contribution to the reduction of the amount of chaos which exists in the interpersonal world. The great inner psychological freedom arising from the readiness to establish autonomous domination over circumstance creates a need for feeling attachments which is channeled into esthetic experience. Artistic self-expression cannot flourish merely on the basis of technique evolving from the mutual identification of artists, but must find an involvement with the sources of human feeling which is worthy of the potential for dominance in the artist, leading on to an exploitation of resources of sufficient scope to produce lasting mastery. Beauty cannot be brought into being by the artificial elaboration of techniques in contexts where there is no commitment to the resolution of the disordered and the chaotic. Inventive manipulation can only create things of value when men are guided by the inner discipline which greatness of human purpose bestows.

Philosophy and art are the vehicle of a creative interaction between the individual and society. Without depth of character elaborated in the personal life of the thinker, his philosophical preoccupations cannot reach an expanding relationship with the world. Under these conditions analytic thinking becomes an exercise in concept manipulation for

its own sake, which is quite different from truth seeking
for its own sake. Without vigor of character which is developed in the personal life of the man of action, his
artistic self-expression cannot reach an expanding relationship with the world. Under these conditions inventive
experimentation becomes a technical exercise which seeks
the development of formal proficiency for its own sake,
which is quite different from adherence to the right for
its own sake.

Philosophy and art have human roots of an elemental
kind. When they leave their origins behind, they fail to
contribute to the growth of individuals and to the effort
of all men to make progress against the unknown and the
chaotic in human affairs. Although truth and right are
inherently communicable and demonstrable, the creative
search for truth and right may carry the individual beyond
the range of the sight and the capacity to participate of
those around him. In the midst of such aloneness and
separateness, the creative individual has to know what is
communicable and demonstrable in terms of his inner
experiences with ideas and methods. He cannot depend on
the response of those who cannot enter the psychological
contexts where the truth and the right can be seen and
experienced. Maturity has no commitment to enter any
context which does not serve its own adaptive purposes.
Society makes a place for its creative members, but it cannot provide them with a guarantee of understanding and
recognition. The individual who is creative enough to think
and act for himself must also be capable of choosing those
contexts in which he will allow his productivity to expose
him to a need for empathy and identification. If the individual lowers the barriers against these needs inappropri-
ately, seeking adaptive rewards for personal attainments
which are essentially creative in structure, he exposes him-

self to extremes of fear and rage which bring his capacity for survival into question.

HUMAN SCIENCE AND ENGINEERING

The historical evolution of man's creative thinking faculties from their origin in religious beliefs, through the development of philosophy, and into systems of pure scientific insight, has been won at the price of losing involvement with the first subject matter of man's search for knowledge, his own psychological nature. Science thrives in a context where it can use pure analytic symbols and can deal with an impersonal world subject to experimentation. An impersonal subject matter does not commit the scientist to any degree of self-exposure for which he is not prepared. The capacity of the right to demonstrate its inevitable workability among all alternatives has reached a high degree of expression in modern engineering accomplishments. There is a historical development of man's capacity for domination of his environment, taking origin in the warrior's skills and developing through the systematic techniques of the artist into modern engineering methods. Involvement with the impersonal resources of the builder's world spares the individual from committing himself to a scope in human undertakings which brings a threat to his self-control.

The development of science and engineering has brought so much expansion of knowledge and ability which are accessible to all men that the rate of change in adaptive life has been greatly accelerated. This kind of material social progress rests on the basis of the creative contributions of individuals, but the emphasis on the development of impersonal knowledge and instrumentalities of power tends to efface the individual search for human meanings and values. Man's creative potential reaches only a partial expression in his scientific accomplishments and in his engineering feats. The more the face of his world is changed by the practical applications of his new insights and mastery, the more the demands of his mature psychological life take on an arbitrary and tyrannical aspect, as if his ideas and techniques had brought a Frankenstein's monster into being that no longer could be kept in a harmonious relationship with his whole psychic life. Rebellion and heresy directed against scientific method and industrial efficiency as a means of making more room for human understanding and responsibility bring a depreciation of adaptive maturity which undermines social stability and adds nothing to man's search for his own soul. It is not the elaborations of maturity which are man's enemy, but the lack of a science of human nature adequate to his needs for universal communication, and the lack of procedures for reliable social control having continuity in any human situation.

Modern psychological science has developed in an artificial way because its roots do not lie in the historical search of civilized man for human truth. Insofar as modern psychological understanding has a scientific structure, it has modeled itself after the successes of scientific thought in the non-human areas. If these models are followed too closely the unique problems of a psychology of the personality fail to be recognized, especially in regard to the personal involvement of the observer with his subject matter at the level of the growth processes. Most of what passes for psychological science is a collection of intuitive beliefs which have meaning only in the specialized contexts in which they were evolved. The great expansion of awareness of the personality in the twentieth century has come primarily through the work of psychotherapists whose preoccupation with the healing of mental illness has guided their observations and brought them the means of testing their hypotheses.

Unfortunately the success of therapeutic manipulations in reducing symptoms is an extremely poor method of validating psychological insights into the nature of the total personality. The pooled intuitive beliefs of psychotherapists have a cultistic structure in which communication is not only limited by private semantic assumptions but more significantly fails to reach society in general at those levels of personal growth where insights are most needed. Modern psychotherapeutic thinking has expanded the awareness of the personality, but it has done little to decrease the unknown in the area of creative interpersonal relationships and has therefore increased the sense of psychological crisis which exists in a world of rapid social change.

The expansion of modern welfare systems has utilized individual contributions of a creative nature, but the social institutions which have evolved from man's increasing determination to take more responsibility for his fellow men do not give direct expression to the historical search for a personal capacity to embody the right. The modern sense of social responsibility follows pathways which have evolved in the impersonal areas of mass production industry. The needs of human beings are met in contexts where political pressures occur, and the scope of these needs is limited to basic survival requirements without genuine regard for the psychological growth strivings of individuals. When there is security in the area of basic necessities the reaching for genuine opportunities in interpersonal relationships increases, and social welfare systems do little to reduce the chaotic quality of these psychological experiences. This failure results in an increase in the sense of crisis which characterizes a world of rapid social change.

TEACHING AND LEADERSHIP IN EDUCATION

The heritage of knowledge which is passed on to the

individual through education prepares him for both adaptive maturity and for handling the impact of the unknown and the chaotic as they emerge in the growth processes. Insofar as education goes beyond the limited functions of teaching basic rudiments or providing the professional and technical knowledge required for a specialized career, it broadens the base of the individual autonomy in dealing with life, increasing the self-awareness and self-confidence of the individual. College education is especially concerned with providing a background for the elaboration of psychological growth, assisting the individual in severing his dependence on familial ideas and modes of behavior. This must be done without a provocative challenge to the established maturity functions of family life. The process requires a psychological hiatus wherein the individual stands in an adolescent position between the old dependence and the coming acceptance of new familial involvements chosen by himself, finding enough time, space, and psychological resources to establish a genuine inner identity of a creative kind. This difficult and hazardous psychological undertaking taxes his capacity for sustaining tensions and mobilizing energies, increasing his exposure to the influence of outside sources of wisdom and strength. Education is expected to provide the kind of teaching and leadership which not only reinforces the growing creative independence of the student but meets his needs for dependent assistance in those areas where the search for inner balance requires it. The gratification of dependent needs in a growing individual has the function of releasing his independent strivings and cannot be allowed to replace the primary goal. If education is to perform this complex function it must provide access to the kind of truth and right which have genuine meaning and value in the area of creative interpersonal relationships. No matter how impressive the qualifications of a community of scholars may be, if they do not bring to their educational task an established body of insights and modalities of mastery which reach the student at the level where his human needs exist, education becomes only another instrument of an already encroaching adaptive maturity, destructive to the very growth process to which it pays formal obeisance.

The exposure of the individual to a psychological climate favorable to growth involves reaching for knowledge and ability for their own sake, as part of a process of self-development. The individual tests the benefits of education in this aspect of his needs by the degree of his awareness of an increasing inner security or by his increasing capacity for inner freedom in relating himself to opportunity. If these advantages are not forthcoming, the enthusiasm and inspiration inherent in the educational process die, leaving only the routine tasks of preparation for adaptive social roles. The struggle against the depressive consequences of this abandonment of the search for an inner identity is a large part of the psychic life of the adolescent personality.

The educational system is ultimately a social institution which must remain stable. Education can rise to no higher a level of function than the established access to truth and right in the community makes possible. Teaching and leadership within the area of the growth processes must reach a direct communicability if the student is to learn, and a capacity for demonstrability which attracts unqualified identification if the student is to accept the example of others. In the world of the private and separate which is the birthplace of man's creative psychological life, there is no guaranteed access to an interpersonal context from which either communicability or demonstrability will flow. Therefore any individual whose psychological involvements are primarily creative in nature will not find himself always at home in the academic world. Conflicts between the individual and the educational system are no different than the

194   LOVE AND POWER

conflicts with any conventional social institution and must
come into the open when the individual has needs which
are greater than the system can supply. Education accepts
a greater awareness of these conflicts and is more exposed
to their influence than other social institutions because of
its commitment to a growth protecting function. When the
individual search for truth and right seeks to use the educational system as a community for personal self-discovery,
ignoring its adaptive function, this effort does violence to
the institutionalized nature of education. A good educational
system makes room for inner security and freedom in the
same sense that a democratic government protects civil
liberties. The system cannot accept alteration by the new
aspects of truth and right that are emerging at any given
time and place unless society itself is being altered by such
influences. The creative person must resist the influences
of the educational system in the same way that he rejects
any automatic incorporation of himself in adaptive undertakings.

In the non-human fields, the resistance of the individual
to incorporation by the educational system is a lesser matter.
The privacy and separateness of the creative process can
be stimulated and protected without committing the individual to any major deviations in his conformity to adaptive
patterns. The educational system provides a simplified
human environment in which the important sources of
human conflict need not have a direct impact on the personality. To some degree the university duplicates the withdrawal inherent in the monastic life in its intellectual aspect,
and duplicates the indifference of the barracks type of living
in its gregarious function. Withdrawal is not the same thing
as privacy, nor is indifference equivalent to a genuine separateness. Once withdrawal has established itself as a necessary element in inner security, the individual no longer has
access to the totality of experience which human truth

requires. Once indifference becomes the key to inner freedom through its capacity to protect the individual from involvements, he can no longer find the elements of permanence in his human attachments which adherence to the right requires. The proper workshop for the expansion of human truth and right lies in an environment chosen by the individual himself, with the fullest access to human selectivity and mobility in his interpersonal relationships, taking its being within a life of adaptive maturity which is kept as simple as possible. Society cannot be expected to provide institutionalized protection for such personal and individual undertakings.

The educational system cannot produce the human insights and mastery that it needs out of its own reservoir of intellectual and procedural assets. The student who exposes himself to higher education with the expectation of finding his soul out of his relationship with the teaching and leadership that the university provides can only end in the disillusionment and bitterness which the failure of expected miracles must bring. Education is an area of social life which will always remain sensitive and helpful to the growth tendencies of individuals, but no one can outgrow the truth or right to which he has access. Since most men need more access to human truth and right than they possess, they must either endure the consequences or set forth on their own to make their independent contributions to mankind's store of human knowledge and ability. There is no guarantee that their efforts will find a worthy harvest at any given time or place, and men cannot use insights and mastery which are being sought but have not yet been found. This means a passage through much human territory that is vague in outline, inarticulate, and perhaps untenable. It is within the atmosphere of such psychological undertakings that many students make a precarious and unstable adjustment to the adaptive aspects of higher education.

PSYCHOLOGICAL SCIENCE AND
SOCIAL CONTROL

The accomplishments of modern science and engineering have evolved from a productive interaction between theory and empiricism. The development of man's conceptual capacities has provided him with intellectual resources which he has applied to the concrete subject matter revealed by empiricism. In the evolution of his identity as an artisan, he has gradually accumulated inventive capacities which have come to great productivity in the modern industrial world through the exploitation of a world of opportunity revealed by scientific theory. When the area of productivity lies outside the human field, the thinker can become a scientist and the man of action can develop his engineering capacities without major stresses in interpersonal relationships. Genuine empiricism for the seeker of human truth cannot be attained if he confines his efforts to a circumscribed area of scientific investigation which leaves his personal life untouched, nor can the seeker of the right in human relationships find a way to establish systems of control without risking his personal identity in the process. Creativity alters the view of life and the way of life of those individuals who undertake the winning of territory from the unknown and the chaotic in interpersonal relationships. If man is to attain a view of his own nature of sufficient scope to reach the generality necessary for a scientific system of ideas, he must live in such a way that he can perceive the true nature of the human events which make up the world around him. No amount of intuitive ingenuity can bring a scientific system out of fragmentary observations which are allowed to usurp the place of an entire whole. It is the exposure of the thinker to an expanding human world which brings him to the point where he can distinguish truth from self-serving beliefs through his capacity to bring unity to his subject matter. If unity is won through compulsive intellectuality and willful exclusion of data he is no longer able to sustain the idealization which alone can bring new insights into being.

In the reaching for a higher level of right in human affairs, the individual must attain permanence in modes of procedure so that techniques can be passed on from one individual to another. The only way that he can discover the actual nature of the human resources which he seeks to develop and control is through the flexibility of his own life, responding to opportunity with an expanding capacity to take advantage of circumstances. No amount of inventive shrewdness can find permanent modes of control in the absence of the ability to explore all aspects of reality. The involvement of the man of action by the human world brings him those critical experiences which make it possible to distinguish between the right and those methods which serve his egotism in the moment, and he does this by testing the continuity of his control in any and all circumstances. If a sense of permanence is won by obsessive elaborations of technique and self-conscious adherence to a restricted aspect of the environment, he is no longer able to sustain the objective sense of reality which alone can bring new mastery into being.

Psychological knowledge is a tool which brings love into interpersonal relationships and not only changes the personality of the thinker but opens the channels of growth in others through its innate communicability. As the lives of groups of individuals are altered by the recognition of new truth, pressure is exerted for social change. Psychological knowledge which is distorted by compulsive mechanisms is readily diverted from its growth serving function to become a part of the building of an aggressive type of maturity. Partial insights into the inner psychic life of others can easily become a destructive force in interpersonal relationships, weakening the cohesive ties when they are needed most. An active state of psychological growth is accompanied by a relatively large investment in what is hidden and private in relationship to the world of maturity, bringing a vulnerability to inferiority feeling. The invasion of this privacy in the name of psychological insight can disrupt the inner security of the individual, exposing him to a growing fear and hate which threatens his basic capacity to feel love in his mature relationships.

The capacity for self-control in any and all human contexts is a tool which brings power into interpersonal relationships. The elaboration of the ability to take responsibility not only changes the personality of the man of action but opens the channels of growth in others through its inherent influence on their approach to experience. As the lives of groups of individuals are altered by the acceptance of new right, pressure is exerted toward change in social institutions. When the capacity for human involvement is distorted by obsessive mechanisms, it is easily diverted from its growth serving function to become an element in the elaboration of a passive type of maturity. Episodic mastery which is not built on lasting attachments can readily undermine the sense of importance as it operates in human affairs, weakening the cooperation of men when it is most needed. As the power capacities expand, there is a relatively large investment in the kind of interpersonal relationships which are dissociated from the world of maturity and which have an accompanying tendency toward a sense of guilt. If the individual gives up this separateness in the name of social responsibility, his inner freedom will be compromised, exposing him to a growing rage and anger which threatens his basic capacity for personal power in his mature relationships.

The search for a science of human nature must be guided by love if it is to avoid compulsive deterioration of the intellectual mechanisms it utilizes. Creative love which seeks knowledge for its own sake, unalloyed by the influence of beliefs which serve the interests of the adaptive life of maturity, is the only pathway to a genuinely submissive relationship to the world of human experience. If this degree of submissiveness were to enter the life of maturity, it would unbalance the individual and destroy his adaptive effectiveness. Man cannot utilize or tolerate the expression of the full range of his love capacities in the market place of daily living. He is creative in his interpersonal relationships when he succeeds in holding the demands of maturity at bay, finding his inner love identity in those human contexts where the work of love can proceed without arbitrary limit. Men who approach maturity with an established capacity for growth will apply their insights to the life of maturity when and where they can. They do not distort their mature relationships by requiring that their love capacities find a full expression there, nor do they lay aside the search for truth because the world does not provide them with automatic rewards for their efforts. The creative individual finds his rewards out of inner experiences, and even though he might at times seem to need a utopia for his psychological undertakings, he actually brings what he needs into being out of his own independent responsiveness to life. A basic requirement for an adequate psychological adjustment to the civilized world is access to the communicable insights by which men make a workable fusion between creativity and maturity. If these insights are not sufficient to perform their task, an inner conflict between growth and maturity will exhaust the psychological productivity of the individual.

The search for modalities of social control must find the pathways developed by personal power if it is to avoid the obsessive entanglements which come from adaptive influences. Creative power which brings ability into existence for its own sake, unbounded by the conventional patterns of

action which maturity requires, is essential to the maintenance of a consistently dominant relationship to the world
of human feeling. If this kind of total dominance is injected
into the life of maturity, it unbalances the individual and
makes antisocial behavior inevitable. Man exhausts himself
in provocative relationships when he attempts to find a
permanent outlet for personal power in daily adaptive
activities. His creativity finds its proper and necessary place
when he keeps his adaptive life in the restricted area where
it belongs, leaving him free to find his inner power identity
in those human contexts where the attachments of power
do not encounter pre-established barriers. As new mastery
develops in the creative personality, it will be applied to
the life of maturity when reality permits, but never at the
cost of the disruption of adaptive adequacy. The creative
individual does not ask the world to change in order to
facilitate his self-fulfillment, but he does maintain without
compromise an unalterable inner identity which exists above
and beyond the circumstances of daily adaptive life. Even
though this relationship to the world might seem to require
unique and special opportunities, he provides for his needs
by becoming the keeper of his own world of resources,
uncovering new aspects of reality through his dominant relationship with life. He must bring to his psychological
adjustment sufficient access to established modalities of
mastery so that the tools he needs for a fusion between
creativity and maturity will be at hand when they are
needed. Unless such human skills are the property of all
men, their growth struggles will only exhaust their psychological productivity.

PSYCHOTHERAPY AND SOCIAL WELFARE

A science of human nature must concern itself with the
growth struggles of the individual, seen in terms of the

dynamic stresses which occur between the creative and adaptive processes as they express themselves throughout a lifetime. Anything less than this kind of totality in the analysis of any individual's psychic life sacrifices the integrity of its subject matter and becomes a potential threat to the harmonious self-awareness of the personality. The development of modern psychoanalysis has been influenced by the empirical model of nineteenth century science. Because psychoanalysis emerged as a medical specialty concerned with the healing of the sick, it focused its attention on the pathological processes arising from the disruption of the adaptive capacities, and this subject matter was taken to be the totality of significant information concerning the structure of the personality. The diagnosis and treatment of mental illness is, however, a poor basis for the empiricism which a basic science requires. Mental illness, when it is seen in terms of the symptoms and syndromes which come to the attention of the psychotherapist, presents a picture of the personality which is readily fragmented and distorted out of proportion. The acceptance of therapeutic success as a test of the validity of insights constitutes a concession to the practical goals of the physician which completely undermines any consistent search for truth for its own sake.

As men expand the interface on which human involvements are based, they must face the psychological consequences of an increasing awareness of each other. There is no such thing as an expanding understanding which does not generate love between people. Love of an impersonal subject matter does not alter its nature. The scientific thinker in the impersonal fields can invest himself without limit in the search for truth without having to deal with changes wrought by his own devotion and faith. The ability to accept the consequences of growth in the area of love feelings is essential to the undertaking of the search for human truth for its own sake. In psychotherapy, the impact of love feelings, technically called the transference, is held under some degree of control by the artificial device of interpreting the patient's feelings while establishing barriers to the psychological exposure of the therapist. The therapist is supposed to come to the relationship fully endowed with a stable set of established insights which will be adequate in a practical sense to any application which the patient's needs will require. The patient, on the other hand, is supposed to limit his interaction with the therapist to the areas where he is aware of psychic pain or where the therapist accepts communication in the name of therapeutic technique. If everything else is carefully excluded, neither participant will be called on to deal with areas of the unknown in themselves which would require creative personal investment.

The maintenance of an artificial barrier between patient and therapist was facilitated by Freud's invention of the couch technique, in which the therapist sits outside the patient's line of vision and the patient expresses himself through the so-called free association. The invisibility of the therapist reduces him to anonymity except when he speaks, and the flow of fragmented thoughts deprives the patient of that autonomous search for meaning which guides all investigations of the unknown. This reduction of the patient to the status of a producer of thought images, fantasies, and emotionally charged fragments of responsiveness for the period of the treatment session provides the therapist with psychological data in which the intuitive search for meaning can take flight without the discipline of the experiential impact which interpersonal involvement brings. This type of analysis, resourceful though it may be in providing help to the patient in dealing with particular aspects of psychic pain and suffering, cannot lead to a unified comprehension of human nature, as the lack of communicability of the resultant insights demonstrates. Not only has the vision of human truth which psychoanalysis has offered failed to reach the daily life of humanity in any way which can lead to a significant reduction of the unknown and the chaotic in civilized living, but the lack of communication among analysts remains notable, although often a well kept secret from the public in general. Many therapists work in their own isolated cell of compulsively arranged psychological wisdom, like a machine which has been programmed to deliver an orderly series of insights when the patient's psychological productivity pushes the right button. Artificially constructed concepts with no consistent relationship to experience flourish like weeds in such an atmosphere.

As long as psychotherapy concerns itself with the relief of psychic distress, avoiding the larger questions which arise from involvement with the creative process, it can perform its medical healing function without doing major violence to the social assets which creativity supplies. Within the restricted world of its therapeutic operations, psychoanalysis is free to build any set of insights it wishes, judging their validity only in terms of their usefulness in reducing psychic pain. The kind of understanding which shows itself to be useful varies tremendously among therapists, depending on the type of human difficulties the individual therapist chooses to make his sphere of concern. He is guided in this choice by the necessity of maintaining the privacy of his own inner identity, and he cannot deal effectively with human problems where he cannot avoid self-revelation. The patient, on the other hand, must be capable of accepting the world of psychic investigation established for him by the analyst, and this requires a blind faith in the therapeutic process. Such faith must generate love but the love for the therapist has literally nowhere to go, since the expanding awareness which love brings is blocked by the technique of therapy itself, leading to a ready sexualization of the attachment. This pathological arrangement teaches many patients that love is dangerous to their personalities. The resultant turning away from further involvement with the growth processes may lead to a more or less successful investment of the self in maturity goals and this often constitutes the therapeutic success. The physician earns his fee, and the patient looks forward to a future of reduced psychic disability. As the impact of the patient's new maturity begins to exact its price throughout the years of its elaboration and development, the lost access to depth undermines harmonious self-awareness and inner security, bringing psychosomatic stresses and depressive phenomena. Psychoanalysts do not keep statistics on these later complications, being fully preoccupied with the emotional crises of their current patients. Therapeutic successes which undermine the autonomous search for truth in human affairs not only lead the individual to settle for less than he could have if an established body of socially communicable insights were available to him, but they subtract his contribution from mankind's effort to make a better world for all men. When the performance of the therapeutic task is guided by the need to reduce disabling symptoms to a manageable level, there can be no quarrel with its goals, but the therapist must not be allowed to use the prestige of his healer's role to endow his capacity for understanding with an aura of wisdom which is fraudulent.

If men are to find their way through the vicissitudes of growth in an autonomous fashion, they will need access to both truth and right in human affairs. The development of a science of human nature can only flourish where men are able to establish new standards of ethical behavior which have an objective existence, leading to an expansion without pre-established limits in man's capacity to take responsibility for the welfare of his own kind. When morality is extending its scope farther and wider in interpersonal relationships, men are able to enter personal growth with an assured source of inner integrity, reinforced by identification with others. These modalities of mutual control which men share together constitute a form of systematic mastery similar to engineering in the non-human fields. There can be no victories over the chaotic in human nature without the expansion of ethical capacities in this objective way. An expanding capacity for love among men needs the ideals which only morality can supply. As personal power expands and brings men into new areas of involvement with each other, they need the enrichment of opportunity which only love can supply.

As men become increasingly involved in new aspects of each other's lives, they cannot avoid the psychological consequences of the development and reinforcement of the self-confidence which such relationships bring. There is no such thing as an expanding capacity for interpersonal responsibility which does not generate power loyalties. Power over impersonal resources deals with a reality which does not change as a consequence of being used. The individual who undertakes to embody the right in human relationships for its own sake must be able to accept the consequences of his own personal growth in the process, dealing with the stresses which develop in his mature social roles. The striving toward an increased responsibility for the welfare of others expresses itself in its most advanced form in the modern emphasis on social service, directed toward the upgrading of the life circumstances of backward individuals and groups in a missionary spirit. The resulting interpersonal relationships tend to carry the participants into an adolescent type of creative growth unless they are isolated through the establishment of an impersonal professional function based on the submissive helplessness of those in need. Mastery in human relationships can develop out of the use of highly developed social techniques which enlarge the scope of the needs of others, leaving them dependent on the giver

of such bounty. This is not the genuine leadership which
evolves from the reaching for the right among equals.
Through the confinement of such involvements to professional channels, the individual has the means of withholding himself from relationships at any point where his
lack of capacity for dealing with the total identity of another
person would be exposed. He acts only through his established modalities of control in contexts where his effectiveness is assured, remaining indifferent to anything else. Such
mastery can never attain the permanence of the right and
cannot become the property of all men. Contributions to
the welfare of others which do not preserve the dignity and
integrity of the recipients cannot reduce the chaotic in
human relationships. The more individuals become dependent on this kind of help, the more their capacity for moral
independence is undermined, leading to an invasion of
their power strivings by inappropriate celebrative phenomena.

ADOLESCENCE AND SOCIAL PROGRESS

The adolescent growth phase of yielding personalities
deepens the love capacities and commits the individual to
a search for an ideal which is worthy of the submissive tendencies in himself. Without the involvement in the service
of an ideal there is no way to avoid perverse deterioration
of the love tendencies. The adolescent growth of assertive
personalities invigorates the power capacities of the self
and commits the individual to a search for a real world of
opportunity which he can match to his emerging dominance. Without the responsiveness of an environment which
is open to being possessed, there is no way to maintain the
self-control which puts aside addiction phenomena.

In a world which lacks adequate human insights and
mastery there is always a potential conflict between growth

and maturity. Each aspect of the psychological life finds elements in the other which threaten its existence. It is typical of the intellectual development of adolescence that it exposes the false idealism which it has inherited, whereas maturity attempts to ignore the importance of new ideas, attempting to draw the adolescent into the conventional commitments which carry their own impelling gratifications. When the growth process must gain its identity through a systematic discrediting of the value of maturity, the search for truth ends in polemics and gives way to provocative rebellion. This kind of anger against social institutions expresses itself toward the stable power structure of society and tends to focus in the political area, choosing those aspects of the political life where the failure of society to attain social justice is most evident. The more rebellious the individual becomes, the more he sacrifices the privacy of his own personal search for human understanding, and the less capable he becomes of sustaining the faith in mankind on which creative love rests.

The reaching of the adolescent for genuine opportunity always tends to threaten the established beliefs which have been inherited from the previous generation. The mature world is committed to modalities of behavior which gain their stability by taking principles for granted, entirely apart from whether they are responsive to the needs of growing individuals or not. When the conventional social roles are pushed aside out of a general refusal to believe in established social meanings, the growth process takes on a heretical identity, and the reaching for a higher development of the right ends in the cultivation of contempt for the general inadequacy of man's social philosophy. Hatred is encouraged against those who are the spokesmen for the socially acceptable humanistic viewpoint of their time since these the disappointment of the heretical individual in the shal- individuals provide the best target for the expression of

lowness of the human environment. The more the individual becomes involved in the intellectual task of depreci-
ating the spiritual forces at work in society, especially in
terms of their indifference to man's personal freedom, the
more he sacrifices the separateness of his own constructive
search for human responsibility, and the less capable he
becomes of sustaining the hope for a better world on which
creative power rests.

The attempt of the adolescent to change the world which
he has inherited from adults becomes an emergency type
of reaction which undermines his search for a growing inner
identity. These psychological stresses between the old and
the new generation can only be handled creatively when
the adolescent is able to limit his involvement in the adaptive world around him. Rebellion and heresy widen the
interface of the interaction with the mature world. The
educational system helps to delay the commitment to a
mature life, but when education is seen as merely a preparation for a more successful participation in conventional
social roles, the coming to an end of the student status
precipitates the individual into an all encompassing involvement with adaptive demands. If the individual comes to the
adaptive world with a depth of love which he cannot use,
he must either attempt to idealize others in contexts where
idealization becomes impossible, or he must rebel and
become an onlooker who watches his own love capacities
ebb away in a struggle where depth no longer has any
meaning. If he attempts to bring his full power capacities
to his adaptive life, he is driven to find a range of opportunity which the mature world cannot supply. If he takes
a heretical path as a result, he will lose interest in the kind
of responsible participation with others which is the only
way that personal power can maintain and express itself.

The rebellious adolescent discovers the immorality of
the world in the form of a personal revelation to him and

his kind which he feels sets him apart from all men who have ever lived. The awareness of the continuity of man's creative struggle to deal with social injustice is lost to him in that moment, and his own autonomous self-awareness shrinks under the influence of his commitment to social action. He no longer pursues truth for its own sake, but maintains a pseudo-individuality through the identity which comes from political protest. Such activities are constructive only insofar as they are truly political in nature, putting pressure on social institutions to evolve toward a new stable equilibrium. The political life of man is one of his most mature activities, and involvement in it at a constructive level cannot become a vehicle for the elaboration of an inner identity. Insofar as the growing personality of the intellectual concentrates its sense of individuality on the attempt to undermine social evils through political action, it loses awareness of its primary challenge which is to deal with the failures of love in the civilized world. The capacity of men to take responsibility for each other cannot outrun their ability to bring creative love into each other's lives.

The heretical adolescent who refuses to believe in the principles which are at the advancing edge of social progress is giving expression to his fundamental dissatisfaction with the forces of shallowness and ignorance in the human world. He undertakes to unmask those who usurp the function of wisdom, losing awareness of the historical continuity of man's devotion to the finding of genuine human truth in the process. In turning toward polemic rejection of the influence of man's intellectual life, he loses access to the autonomous self-confidence which depends on the love of others. He no longer reaches for the right for its own sake, but maintains a pseudo-individuality through his role in the cultivation of hatred among social groups. Such activities can only be constructive when they are brought into the open through a mature participation in political conflict, becoming an influence on the emerging nature of social ideas in a world in progress. Although hatred for that which is false is an essential element in man's political life, the personality of the man of action cannot find the basis for independent growth in its rejection of intellectual influences, false though they may be in many contexts. The individual must maintain involvement with his primary personal goal, which is to deal with the inadequacies of power in the civilized world.

Love cannot develop creatively without an attachment to a worthy ideal. Anger at injustice, no matter how valid the emotion may be in the context it occurs, does not provide the idealism which the work of faith requires. The recognition of injustice is easily gained by merely looking at the world as it is. To know the nature of justice in the total scope of man's experiential world is a task which only love is fit to undertake. Power cannot develop creatively without involvement in a world of opportunity which is measured to its potentials. Hatred for intellectual dishonesty, no matter how valid the emotion may be in the contexts which arouse it, cannot provide the awareness of a responsive environment which alone can sustain hope in its reaching for fulfillment. Ignorance masquerading as truth is readily encountered in civilized man's interpersonal relationships, but the identification and exploitation of genuine human knowledge is a task which only personal power is fit to undertake.

CREATIVITY AND SOCIAL INSTABILITY

The search for truth in human affairs exposes the yielding personality to a self-awareness which develops as an end in itself, just as the need to embody the right in human affairs develops a self-confidence in the assertive personality which pursues its own course. This internal growth of the self finds any outlet and expression which its own expansion dictates, using honesty and courage as its tools, and it cannot be confined by the image of the self which comes from the social roles of family life and the adaptive world.

Once the individual has left behind the relatively unstructured relationship to maturity which is his privilege in adolescence, he enters a world of increasingly stable mature commitments which resist new efforts at inner growth and the accompanying alterations in his self-image. Honesty and courage come easily to the young; major growth efforts which come in the midst of mature commitments must cost the individual a great deal in terms of conventional adaptive efficiency. There is no inherent or inevitable conflict between the psychological growth forces and the stable equilibrium of maturity. The conflict develops when the creative individual cannot maintain the autonomy which growth requires and he must therefore attempt to undermine social ideas and institutions as an outlet for his personal search for an inner identity. Society contributes equally to the conflict when it fails to respect the privacy and separateness of the creative interpersonal life of individuals, finding distaste and danger in psychological phenomena which should be of no concern to the representatives of stable law and authority in social life.

The fear and rage reactions of society toward its deviant elements produce invasive emergency responses which reduce both social stability and the constructiveness of growth efforts of individuals. It is difficult for society to avoid intrusion into the areas of personal growth when the adolescent phases of development seek rebellious and heretical outlets. It is equally difficult for the growing individual to confine his search for truth and right to those areas which are not involved with his adaptive life, especially since maturity spreads its influence into the core of his person-

ality by its acceptance and sponsorship of perverse and
addicted elements in interpersonal relationships. In a progressive society there is no actual requirement that the individual accept the ignorance and immorality that are taken
for granted among men in their adaptive life, but it sets
goals of social accomplishment and mutual acceptance
which cannot be reached by those who are honest and
courageous in their personal relationships. The individual
must therefore pay the price of a diminution of his conventional security and freedom if he is to find the kind of
inner security and freedom which comes out of his own
individual self-expression. The ultimate hold which maturity
uses to encroach on the personal psychological life of individuals consists of its capacity to undermine the enthusiasm
and inspiration of the growth processes by substituting
conventional ambition for inner development. It accomplishes this end by rendering the individual ignorant of
the choices he is making, setting itself against creative self-
knowledge and sponsoring the socially accepted understanding which draws him into the shared perversity that men
think they must have in order to empathize with each
other. The mature world also guides the individual away
from the utilization of autonomous self-control without his
making a recognizable choice. It substitutes dependence on
the socially accepted patterns of responsibility which reinforce his power posture through addicted mechanisms, without which men risk the lack of mutual identification.

As long as men overinvest themselves in their mature
adaptive life, they will require the extra rewards which
come from self-aggrandizing love and the vanity of pretentious power. Without this systematic cultivation of appetites and interests which can be gratified only by turning
away from the highest levels of human truth and right, they
must fail to hold the menace of their depressive tendencies
at bay. Those who see the ignorance that surrounds them

in the human scene, and those who choose to accept a personal concern with the immorality in their environment, must turn away from the seduction and intimidation inherent in the rewards of maturity. The price they pay for their independence includes exposure to the fear of aloneness and to rage at enforced separateness in their interpersonal life. Some individuals are overwhelmed by the disorientation and disorganization that follows. It is sometimes taken to be in the interests of the life of maturity to discredit such individuals, looking on their independence as the source of their incapacities and antisocial tendencies. Such psychological difficulty is no menace to social progress, however, since the psychopathology remains personal and provides society a way to perceive and deal with social problems and obstacles which would otherwise be invisible or ignored. Out of the group of these deviant individuals come some autonomous personalities who make substantial contributions in the struggle against the unknown and the chaotic in human affairs.

The life of maturity brings an inflexibility to the psychological life of man which is fully capable of destroying civilization itself. Acting in the name of wisdom and strength, men commit themselves to social roles which remove them from access to those interpersonal contexts where creative love and power take root and grow. The individual whose depth of character expresses itself exclusively in the attachments of family life and its extensions in the community can never use that depth to bring new insights into human affairs. The more successful he becomes in serving family interests and the more intensely he becomes preoccupied with the love of others who are like himself, the more he loses any capacity to measure the degree of his cynicism and his self-aggrandizing relationship to the total world of man's social experience. In order to preserve his hard won adaptive efficiency, he must use ideas within a limited human world, excluding genuine awareness of any psychological forces which would bring distress to the psychological security that he shares with his own kind. No matter how intuitive, ingenious, and resourceful his manipulation of ideas in the human sphere may be, these ideas must ultimately be the servants of his self-aggrandizing security and not the instruments of a search for the kind of lasting truth which belongs to all men. Both his ability to love and his intellectual capacities are channeled by the need for communication with those he seeks to influence for adaptive purposes. The gratifications which come from such pleasure giving intensifications of his self-awareness cannot avoid contamination by perverse mechanisms. It is perversity which becomes acceptable because it has an adaptive purpose. The more facile he becomes in dispensing love feelings and humanistic ideas the greater is his access to power in his conventional social roles.

The individual who finds an exclusive expression for the vigor of his inner self in familial involvements and their extensions in the community can never use his inner readiness for action to bring new modalities of mastery into being in the human world. The more his sense of ownership becomes focused in family attachments and the more his pride becomes a matter of power partnerships with others like himself, the more he loses any measure of the degree of his opportunism and the extent of the vanity inherent in his loyalties. In order to retain the sense of social conformity which has been laboriously constructed out of a systematic acceptance of principles imposed from without, he must use his human skills only in the prescribed areas, finding a full sense of freedom at the cost of confinement within the kind of human attachments which he is allowed to feel. No matter how inventive, spontaneous, and rewarding his skills may become in establishing immediate influence over others, his ways of taking responsibility must ultimately show themselves to be captive psychological forces, bound to an egotistical type of freedom and unable to establish the kind of moral integrity which all men can imitate. Both his ability to embody personal power and his manipulative social capacities are channeled by the need to attract the cooperation of others for adaptive purposes. The sense of accomplishment which comes from such mood elevating reinforcements of self-confidence cannot avoid being captured by addicted mechanisms. It is a kind of power addiction which becomes acceptable because it serves adaptive needs. The more secure the individual becomes in his power sharing arrangements with others, and the more he functions as the keeper of his brother's pride, the greater is his sense of being loved in the performance of his social roles.

HOMOSEXUALITY AND SOCIAL PROGRESS

Family life is part of man's adaptive world. It utilizes love and power capacities which it does not itself create. Although parents rear children in such a way that the parental character specialization shapes the personality of the child, the creative development of love and power tendencies in adults must find its proper outlet in the outside world. Although the needs and goals of family life are adaptive in nature, the family must make a place for the psychologically surplus phenomena of sex and celebration. It accomplishes this end by utilizing the surpluses in a rational and disciplined way, attaching them to the marital relationship through socially reinforced patterns of feeling and modes of behavior. Once the surpluses are given a socially acceptable place, a psychological struggle ensues to find the necessary depth and spontaneity which alone can make sex and celebration a fulfilling experience. The tendency to incorporate perverse and addicted mechanisms into socially acceptable sex and celebration is very strong, because the primitive mated interaction between masculine and feminine cannot be utilized in family life, and its absence threatens to undermine the sensual commitment and the self-abandonment which the surpluses require.

The independent relationship of the individual to society rests on his creative psychological capacities. No individual can find an autonomous inner identity without character specialization of the yielding or assertive type, which means that the mated mechanisms which are used in nature to form the familial domain are turned to a different use in the civilized world. Psychological femininity and masculinity become the sources of love and power in interpersonal relationships, providing the basis for the search for truth and right. The character specializations employ the mated mechanisms in the relationship of the individual to the world outside, in its permanent and total aspects. The greater the inner need for growth becomes, the greater is the sense of exposure to the unknown and the chaotic in the world. The individual cannot grow unless the world in which he lives grows with him. This does not mean that he attempts to force change on the world, but that he becomes more aware of it and more participant in it.

Character specialization brings an identity to the self which rests on imbalance. As the individual searches for the expression of the other half of his psychological tendencies, he finds himself in a dependent position. To find balance without losing his creative identity, he must be able to make human relationships which belong in a creative context, above and beyond the fabric of interactions which belong to his life of adaptive maturity. Such relationships bring the idealizing tendency of the yielding personality into focus, and release the assertive personality to a full expression of its capacity for exploitation of the responsiveness of others. It is in the unstructured world

of masculine friendships that such relationships gain their
fullest realization. As men find love and power attachments
which are ends in themselves, they give a growing identity
to their inner natures and at the same time provide dependent support for the maintenance of the necessary balance
in each other. The civilized world has difficulty with these
relationships at the level where the sexual and celebrative
tendencies emerge. There is no way to avoid dealing with
surplus tendencies in any relationship between opposites
where love and power have no fixed limits. If men are not
prepared for this psychological task, they must turn away
from such relationships altogether.

Men who cannot handle the awareness of their deep
feminine tendencies must retreat in fear from any context
which would bring these tendencies to expression. The flight
leads directly into the compensatory masculinity of the
social roles. Not only does this state of affairs bring the
possibilities of personal growth to an end, but it elevates
aggressive masculinity into the place which belongs to a
genuine masculine ideal. Men who cannot handle the
expanding self-confidence which comes from an autonomous
masculine vigor must turn away from the contexts which
threaten to mobilize rage within the inner self. This rejection of psychological freedom leads directly into the compensatory feminine submissiveness of the social roles. This
overemphasis on maturity ends the possibilities of personal
growth and substitutes a shallow passive femininity for
the more responsive reality which a genuine feminine
capacity can bring into being.

The path to creative utilization of the yielding tendencies
lies through a self-awareness which requires honesty about
the self. This struggle to be honest brings many individuals
to an awareness of homosexual feeling which is alien to their
sense of their own identity. Homosexual feeling lies outside
the life of adaptive maturity and therefore is properly secret

in relationship to the conventional adaptive functions, but it cannot remain secret from the individual himself if he is to find the capacity for inner growth. The maintenance of a unified self-image in the presence of the homosexual tendencies is the psychological task of first importance for the yielding personality in the civilized world. If this task is avoided by erecting barriers against self-knowledge, the individual becomes committed to those mature contexts in interpersonal relationships which will preserve his ignorance of himself, thus laying the basis for the phenomenon of repression.

The path to creative utilization of the assertive tendencies lies through a self-confidence which requires uncompromising courage in individual self-expression. The struggle to find this kind of freedom brings many individuals to a readiness for gregarious power partnerships with other men in which the celebrative tendencies are mutually reinforced. Such group attitudes arising from a gang spirit are in conflict with the mature image of masculine stability and are properly dissociated in relationship to the conventional adaptive functions, but they cannot remain dissociated within the personality if the individual is to find the capacity for inner growth. The maintenance of the continuity of personal integrity in the presence of the gregarious celebrative tendencies is the psychological task of first importance for the assertive personality in the civilized world. If this challenge is avoided by the erecting of barriers against independent celebrative experience, the individual becomes committed to those mature contexts in interpersonal relationships which make no demands on his personal self-control, thus laying the basis for the phenomenon of renunciation.

If men limit their love capacities by excluding love for its own sake, seeking only to find the kind of love which serves their adaptive needs, they cannot accept the challenge to grow which comes from society's need for social progress. The awareness of the human problems which need solution for the sake of all men depends on a creative surplus within the individual personality. Without this creative surplus, men lack the inner security which they need for their own mental health. Any self-aggrandizing attempt to solve personal problems without an awareness of the problems of others ends in the deterioration of truth seeking, because the thinker cannot sustain the aloneness which underlies the autonomous search for universal human insights. An unlimited and unstructured receptivity to love feelings must pass through those areas of idealization of assertive masculinity which awaken homosexual feeling. Unless men understand, accept, and utilize their homosexual feeling in a creative fashion they are unable to meet the challenging impact of social problems. Because the homosexual feelings bring so much fear of loss of adaptive effectiveness in fulfilling the demands of the masculine social roles, men do not permit love to bring them the kind of experiential involvement with other men which is essential to the growth of the love capacities. It is the barrier against recognition of homosexual feeling which condemns society to the use of magical beliefs in the place of genuine human understanding. The atavistic stupidities in men's comprehension of their psychological natures stand in strange contrast to the intellectual accomplishments of the twentieth century scientific world.

If men accept restriction in their embodiment of personal power through the exclusion of power for its own sake, expressing only those power tendencies which serve their adaptive needs, they cannot maintain the access to growth which social progress requires. The commitment to the overcoming of obstructions in human cooperation depends on a creative surplus within the individual personality. Without this inner surplus, men lack the inner freedom which is essential to the fusion of constructiveness and social conformity. If men attempt to bring an increased capacity for control into human relationships which is limited to their personal adaptive needs, their efforts will undergo an egotistical deterioration of the integrity associated with the right. The individual can only participate in an inventive and experimental search for new mastery in human relationships when he can sustain the autonomous separateness which such activity entails. An unlimited and unstructured expressiveness of power must pass through the areas of human opportunity brought into being by the presence of yielding masculinity in the civilized world. Unless men can find their creative identity through the fullest involvement with the psychologically feminine in the masculine community, they are unable to find the psychological strength which the obstructiveness of human weakness requires. It is when the untrammeled masculine ideal cannot find a home in the civilized world that it forces its way in the channels of sexual promiscuity and anti-intellectual cultism. Because of the threat of diffuse rage reactions at the frustrations of creative masculinity, men protect their adaptive effectiveness by turning toward the established submissiveness of their conventional social roles. This renunciation of the free search for assertive self-expression is made possible by the loss of capacity to feel the depth of the responsiveness of other men. When the ability to exploit the creative love of others dies, the access to growth of the power capacities disappears with it. It is the barrier against involvement with the yielding resources of the masculine community, and the homosexual implications which such attachments bring, that confines the assertive search for heroic self-expression to an impoverished territory which can only provoke miraculous pretense in the elaboration of human responsibility. Man's inadequacy in the handling of interpersonal control stands in marked contrast to the accumulation of skills in the twentieth century world of industrial engineering.

PRESCRIPTION FOR SURVIVAL

The most mature and apparently well adjusted members of society are those who succeed in establishing a fixed relationship to a stable human environment. Anxiety and restlessness can be excluded by turning away from human contexts which require psychological growth, insuring the individual against unfulfilled longings and the vigilant readiness for opportunities which do not lie at hand. This type of stable existence, which can only be won by insulating the individual and his kind from interaction with the unfulfilled needs and strivings of society as a whole, is built on a foundation of self-aggrandizing aggression and passive vanity. If this kind of maturity is to succeed, there must be a rigid exclusion of the interference which comes from the desire to contribute to the building of a better world for all men. The need for a deepening and increasingly vigorous inner identity is held at bay by the elaboration of the rewards of maturity, utilizing material aggrandizement and the sophisticated elaboration of sensuality. Discontent and unhappiness lurk close to the borders of such a life, and human truth and right which would expose the individual to the influence of shame and guilt become the most dangerous of psychological forces.

When men reject this kind of selfish and egotistical complacency in favor of a life guided by love and personal power, they expose themselves to major dislocations in their capacity to reach a mature adjustment. The release of self-awareness which the autonomous search for love brings, and the mobilization of self-confidence which results when power is given untrammeled expression, bring a flood of disorienting and disorganizing psychological phenomena, expos-

ing the individual to the unknown and the chaotic in interpersonal relationships. The life of conventional maturity
provides maps and manuals for the guidance and control of
human understanding and responsibility. When the individual goes outside and beyond the areas where these aids
operate, he has nothing to follow but the inherent sense
of purpose in love, and the inherent capacity of power to
form its own loyalties. If love and power are to take priority
in establishing the view of life and way of life of men, they
must have full access to the flexible interpersonal attachments and interactions which growth requires. Love and
power cannot be embellishments designed to hold the depressive manifestations of maturity at bay, but must come
to the individual in such a way that he is free to follow
wherever they may lead regardless of the consequences.

Civilized man can choose the way he relates himself to
the social life of mankind. It is the scope of his feelings for
other people and the depth of the involvements he accepts
with them that determine the degree of creative personal
investment that he makes. There is no such thing as drawing
back once he has felt and experienced the heightened sense
of individuality which the enthusiasms and inspirations of
creative love and power bring to the inner identity. Man's
greatest psychological possession is his capacity to give to
others in such a way that his wisdom and strength grow
in the process. Peace of mind and spontaneous involvement
in experience are his greatest rewards, and with these sources
of contentment and happiness firmly established within his
personality, he can live his life with the ultimate in self-
realization. Man cannot find the richness of feeling which
comes from a sense of the importance of living and the
elevated mood which accompanies greatness in human purposes without exposing himself to the challenge of making
his personal contribution to the bringing of a better world
into existence. His inner identity rests on his relationship

to the emerging social progress which all men want. This identity arises from the independent choices that he makes in forming interpersonal relationships. The personal rewards which he gains from this creative area of his life provide the motivation for its continuing and widening development. Love and power must grow in relationship to a human world or they lose their meaning and value. Men cannot find honesty outside a psychological context where honesty is a productive vehicle of human interaction. When honesty produces truth which becomes the property of all men it validates itself and provides its own reason for being. Men cannot find courage except in contexts where the need to be courageous comes to the individual without self-conscious choice on his part. When courage leads to the establishment of the right, it becomes an example to all men and provides its own reason for being. Where the commitments of maturity erect barriers against the kind of creative self-investment which bring honesty and courage into being, the development of truth and right in the world comes to an end, and the access to social progress disappears.

The importance and greatness of creative human needs and purposes cannot find their expression in the mature adaptive life of man. It is civilized man's greatest delusion that all that is best in his own nature can be invested in his vocational adjustment, in the warmth and pride of family life, and in his relationship with the established social beliefs and institutions of his day. The best in himself belongs to the realm of truth seeking and the reaching for the right, and this search can only go forward with the necessary continuity and integrity when he involves himself in those human contexts where his surplus love and power capacities are free to find their own destiny, secure in their removal from adaptive requirements. The attempt to find inner growth through the overinvestment of love and power where they are neither needed or wanted only means that the individual must try to love the unlovable and establish control over the inherently intransigent. The more he loves under such conditions, the more he hates, and the more he attempts to give personal expression to a power posture, the more angry he must become. The presence of such hatred and anger dries up the wellsprings of human understanding and responsibility.

Society as a whole is the keeper of its stable social ideas and institutions. In a world of creative maturity society leaves room for the individual to develop an autonomous personal psychological life which is both selective and mobile. In this area the unique individuality of the personality can do its psychological work and find the unlimited expression which creative love and power require. This part of the self is private, but not hidden from the self or others who share it on a similar creative basis, and its experiential components are dissociated from adaptive activities, but can be shared in cooperation with others who have similar goals. The aloneness which comes to privacy in those phases where the individual moves ahead of his fellow men in his love capacities, and the failure of companionship to keep pace with the separateness of the search for personal power, bring the individual to the edge of fear of the death of his emotional life, and to the edge of rage at the prospect of the impoverishment of his human attachments. This emptiness is bridged by faith and hope. The threatening nature of aloneness and separateness does not cause love to turn to hate, nor power to be converted to anger. These psychological forces can retain their permanence and wholeness under such circumstances, ready to fulfill themselves in the finding of truth and right which can then be offered to others in those times and places when they are ready to accept them. Creative love and power are truly independent in that they give without qualification or reservation. They alone can fulfill man's desire to establish something outside himself which is a full expression of the best in himself. The creative human accomplishments are all men will ever know of immortality and utopia, and they are the real sources of what he calls his soul. Civilization itself is still in an adolescent-like phase of development. There is not yet a sufficient reservoir of scientific human truth or demonstrable modalities of human right in the area of social control for the independent individual in a state of growth to find his way through the morass of inhibition and perplexity which he encounters. Those who cannot sustain the onslaught of the disorienting influence of the unknown and the disorganizing effect of the chaotic must turn back. If they escape the disabling consequences of mental illness and antisocial behavior in the process, they are left with a surplus in psychic resources which is inevitably attracted to their adaptive social life. The older generation refuses to recognize the depth of the human ignorance and the scope of the social immorality which results. The younger generation turns toward rebellious and heretical channels of self-expression, generating more hatred and anger in the world because they must challenge the usurpers of their ideals and the betrayers of their opportunities. Truth and right cannot be won in this fashion. The turning against the basic requirements of maturity can only create crises which bring emergency measures into being. The building of a better world is a matter of bringing the tools for the task into existence. Once men have access to the necessary understanding and have developed the means of taking responsibility for each other's fate, there will be no lack of hands and willing hearts to make the necessary changes. Social progress never comes until the human groundwork for it has been laid in the lives of particular individuals. When enough people have deepened their ability to love, and have developed a sufficient scope in their human power capacities, the transition into a truly

wise and moral society will come smoothly, in a world of
men at peace with each other's natures who have put aside
the instruments of their mutual humiliation and provocation.

Man must learn that he has nothing to fear from anything
in his own nature, and this is especially true in the area of
his sexual and celebrative tendencies. His great need to
desexualize creative love and divest creative power of
celebrative contamination does not mean that he can
scorn the sexuality which comes from the growing part of
himself or turn away from the celebrative tendencies which
growth releases. There is a place for everything in human
nature which comes out of man's struggle to find his individuality. The fact that adaptive family life has made a
fixed and stable place for sexuality and celebration does
not mean that the conventional world of adaptive maturity
can exclusively contain all the sexual and celebrative phenomena which come into the lives of human beings. Men
who pursue the path of love are not prepared for the depth
of feminine identity which their growth brings. Men who
seek to embody the creative masculine ideal of the civilized
world are no less overwhelmed by their encounter with the
extremes of their need for feminine response in the masculine
world. Creative masculinity requires the capacity to handle
a heroic type of inner identity which cannot find fulfillment
in adaptive relationships.

The survival of civilization is at stake in the materialistic
and sophisticated twentieth century world which modern
science and industry have brought into being. Man is
burdened with insights which do not tell him what he needs
to know, and embarrassed by modalities of mastery which
bring the threat of mass murder and suicide into the world
of his daily existence. While science and industry are com-
pounding his folly and his knavery, there are other forces at
work above and beyond the circumstances of his daily adap-

tive life, where men are laboring in the vineyards of their private and separate lives, striving to bring the truths into existence which only love can find, and the modalities of the right which only the unflagging devotions of power can discover.

There are no shortcuts to the building of a better world. If fear and rage drive men to enforced changes in their social ideas and institutions, they can only expose themselves to the devastation which loss of stability releases. The responsibility for the struggle against social ignorance and immorality rests on any individual who is capable of sustaining the independent search for truth and right in his own life. It is the individual, however few or however many, who carries the destiny of civilization on his shoulders. There is no census available to men to give them the count of how many of their fellow men have independent access to a creative interpersonal life. Those who cry havoc in the face of the inescapable evidence of man's social immaturity will not share in the task which confronts mankind. Those who enter the ways of love and power only to fall by the wayside will not do harm to their fellow men. There is only one ultimate evil, the cynicism which saps faith, and one ultimate immorality, the opportunism which devastates hope. No advance in truth and right is ever lost, and all the individual has to do to find the importance and greatness which are his human heritage is to give expression to the love that he knows is in his heart, and to the power that his sense of his own proud integrity tells him he possesses.

Life is each human being's workshop. If a man survives a lifetime with his creative capacities intact, he has done his part to make a better world for all men. To do this, he must face a world which is often hostile to the adolescent spirit, reacting to him with a destructiveness born of ignorance and weakness. The stable world of man's established social ideas and institutions is not yet itself mature, lacking as it does the fundamentals of communicable human truth and demonstrable human right. With the advent of each new generation, men increasingly find the psychological resources for the acceptance of the personal task of shaping their own lives, employing standards which they alone choose, and taking the consequences on their own shoulders. There is no room for any other way to live, if civilization is to survive.

The survival of civilization rests on the outcome of the war being waged by the individual against the faithlessness and hopelessness of the established forces of maturity in the civilized world. These are battles in which no blood is shed, nor is any brick dislodged from any wall. It is a war which finds its battlefield in the aloneness of the personal search for understanding, and in the separateness of the personal life which seeks its own kind of responsibility. The battle horn of the intellectual is a call to all men capable of independent thought to expose themselves to the kind of human honesty which alone can bring communicable truth to mankind. The man of action raises a banner for the rallying of those among his brothers who have the ability to face life with the kind of personal courage which alone can put the instrumentalities of the right into the hands of all men. With the gathering clouds of disaster hanging over man's undertaking on earth, the human worth of the individual stands revealed, like the tiny light of a candle in a vast darkness. To your tents, O Israel!

INDEX

Addiction; definition of, 33; adaptive uses, 138; relation to maturity, 171

Adolescence; function of, 30; psychological atmosphere, 54; and the surpluses, 89, 93; and dependence, 89; and character development, 90; and creativity, 90; and growth, 94; delayed maturity, 99; and mated mechanisms, 100; conflict with adults, 106; formation of community, 106; dependency through community, 108; teaching and leadership, 109; education and the community, 110; transition to maturity, 111; and family life, 112; prolonged, 113; and biological maturation, 114; adaptation to surpluses, 115; and unattached surpluses, 117; relation to adults, 117; and political rebellion, 207; and anti-intellectuality, 207; rejection of maturity, 208

Adventuresome spirit, 43

Aggression; definition of, 64; mechanisms of, 68

Analytic thinking; relation to tension holding, 18; basis of, 78; relation to creativity, 81

Anxiety, and phobic state, 72

Art, 187

Assertive character, definition, 17

Balance, personality, 20

Beauty, nature of, 36

Celebration; basis of, 14; mechanisms of, 23; surrender, 23; adjustment, 31, 56; deviations, 55; unattached, 67; and maturity, 87.

Celebrative partnerships; involvements in masculine community, 163; and rage reactions, 167; episodic, 168; community of vagabonds, 172; structure of community of vagabonds, 173; and renunciation, 218; and promiscuity, 220

Chaotic, the, relation to character, 19

Character; specialization, 17, 29; influence of family life, 17

Compulsive mechanism; nature of, 64, 75; relation to obsessive mechanism, 78

Conceptual thinking; see Analytic thinking

Contentment, 179

Courtship, function of, 43

Creativity; basis of, 16; relation to surpluses, 52; relation to shame and guilt, 53

Cultistic experience, 75

Delinquency; and dependency, 73; and heresy, 74; and delayed maturity, 100

Dependence, psychological, 22

Depression; relation to maturity, 60, 97; flattened affect type, 99; retarded mood type, 99; secondary manifestations, 99; and immorality, 178
Dissociation, relation to creative power, 58
Domain, nature of, 14
Dominance, relation to environment, 13

Education; relation to magical and miraculous, 124; function for growth, 192; nature of student needs, 193; as social institution, 193; conflict with individual, 194; relation to withdrawal and indifference, 194; limits in creative function, 195
Emergency reactions, 19
Empathy, 95
Energy retention, 18
Engineering, human; and psychology, 190; failures in welfare systems, 191, 205; relation to power, 199
Enlistment; function of, 63; and masculine community, 155; relation to social progress, 182; and growth, 184; daring undertakings, 184; *esprit de corps,* 187
Equilibrium, unstable, 32
Evil, concept of, 139
Exploitation; nature of, 37; relation to celebration, 38, 87

Faith, function of, 28
Family life; addicted elements, 34; perverse elements, 34; nonmated basis, 34; and idealization, 37; and psychological balance, 37; adaptation to surpluses, 40; dependent mechanisms, 41; and the romantic and adventure-

some spirit, 43; prohibitions and permissiveness, 101; conflicting roles of men and women, 102; balance through social roles, 104; dependent femininity and masculinity, 104; perverse and addicted tendencies, 141; sexual and celebrative adjustment, 169
Fantasy; function of, 49, 125; relation to growth, 49; relation to adolescence, 126
Fear, relation to sexuality, 19
Freud; awareness of sexuality, 140; concept of sin, 141; Freudian id, 141; couch technique and free association, 202
Friendship; and creativity, 147; function of, 148; exclusion of women, 149; mated mechanism, 151; and the social roles, 152; relation to sex and celebration, 152

Gender traits; relation to social roles, 44; flexibility in courtship, 48
Goodness, nature of, 37
Growth, psychological, 21
Guilt; basis of, 51; relation to social roles, 52

Happiness, 180
Heresy; nature of, 74; relation to addiction, 143
Homosexuality; psychological sources, 153; awareness in the masculine community, 162; fear of, 166; unattached, 167; homosexual community, 171; structure of the homosexual community, 172; and compensatory masculinity, 217; and repression, 218; and magical beliefs, 219
Hope, function of, 28

Idealization; relation to inner security, 26; source, 26; nature of, 36; relation to sexuality, 38; self-aggrandizing, 60; and sexuality, 86

Identification, 95

Imbalance, character, 21

Indifference, mechanism of, 36

Independence, psychological, 131

Inferiority, sense of; *see* Shame

Inhibition; and aggression, 70; nature of, 159

Inventive manipulation; basis of, 80; relation to creativity, 82

Love; relation to faith, 27; capacity for idealization, 36; relation to creative goals, 82; relation to growth, 84; empathetic, 95, 121; relation to power union, 119; falling in love, 119

Magic; mechanisms of, 123; and sexuality, 124

Masculine community; psychological function of, 155; and growth, 156; and aggression and passivity, 157; and psychological dependence, 158; creative contexts, 161; growth atmosphere, 166

Mated mechanism, nature of, 16

Maturity; relation to creativity, 64, 96, 97; and depression, 96; and marital adjustment, 101; relation to goodness and beauty, 176

Miraculous behavior; mechanisms of, 123; and celebration, 124

Neurosis; and dependency, 73; and rebellion, 74; and delayed maturity, 100

Normalcy; heterosexual image, 129; community standards, 130; relation to social roles, 134; relation to sexual and celebrative deviation, 135; conflict with creativity, 136

Obsessive mechanism, nature of, 64, 75

Passivity; definition of, 65; mechanisms of, 69

Perplexity; and passivity, 71; nature of, 159

Perversity; definition of, 33; adaptive uses, 138; relation to maturity, 171

Philosophy, 187

Phobic barrier, 72

Phobic state, mechanisms of, 72

Play-acting; function of, 49, 125; relation to growth, 50; relation to adolescence, 126

Power; relation to hope, 28; capacity for exploitation, 36; relation to creative goals, 82; relation to growth, 85; imitative identification, 95, 122; relation to love union, 119; exclusive possession, 120

Privacy, relation to creative life, 57

Psychopathic release, 73

Psychopathic state, mechanisms of, 73

Psychotherapy; cultism in, 191; development of psychoanalysis, 201; limitations for scientific method, 201; nature of transference, 202; failure to understand growth, 203; mechanics of the cure, 204; late depressive complications, 204

Rage, relation to celebration, 19

Reality, sense of; relation to inner freedom, 26; and vanity, 60

Rebellion; nature of, 74; relation to perversity, 143

Restlessness, and psychopathic state, 72

Retreat; function of, 63; and masculine community, 155; relation to social progress, 182; and growth, 183; and parental functions, 183; monastic personality, 186

Right; definition of, 19; and social progress, 61; and celebrative control, 170

Romance, and family life, 43

Scientific method; and human nature, 190; distortions in modern psychology, 190; relation to love, 198; limitations of psychotherapy, 201

Separateness; see Dissociation

Sexuality; basis of, 14; mechanisms of, 23; orgastic, 23; adjustment, 31, 55; deviations, 55; unattached, 66; and maturity, 87

Shame; basis of, 51; relation to social roles, 52

Sin, concept of, 139

Social control; see Engineering, human

Social progress; relation to insight and mastery, 86; and social immaturity, 148

Social roles; masculinity and femininity, 42; and gender traits, 44; feminine stability, 45; masculine stability, 46; in family life, 47

Social service, 205

Submission, relation to environment, 13

Surplus, desexualized and noncelebrative, 24

Tension holding, 18

Transference; nature of, 202; pathological nature, 203

Truth; relation to inner security, 19; and social progress, 61; and sexual knowledge, 170

Unknown, the, relation to character, 19

Withdrawal, mechanism of, 35

Yielding character, definition of, 17